AFRICA
ON A
PIN AND A
PRAYER

BY BOB T. EPSTEIN

Africa on a Pin and a Prayer

Bob T. Epstein, Author/ Publisher

Barbara Epstein, Editor

Copyright © 2013

ISBN-13: 978-1467988919
ISBN-10: 146798891X

Questions about the book contact:

bobepstein@aol.com

"All things have a beginning and end, what is completed between those times is the sum total of the reality of each and every person that is, or has been on this earth. Some few make an indelible mark during their time on earth, while most others leave not even the slightest footnote in history."

- Author

TABLE OF CONTENTS

FORWARD

"I've known Bob Epstein for more than three decades and had encouraged him to write his adventures down for everyone to enjoy and learn from. He has done a wonderful job! I've read part his manuscript and I am proud to say that anyone that is about to embark on his own adventure of a lifetime will feel they are sitting right next to him in his Land Rover as you take the journey with him. This journey took him through parts of Africa including The Congo and more than 12 other countries on the continent and the game parks of East Africa. I more than highly recommend this book to you. I exhort you to read every word of it. This book is a window into a world that is rapidly disappearing, and Bob has captured the essence of this place and has book-marked an adventure for a lifetime."

--Horace Carter, Pulitzer Prize Winner for Literature, CEO Southern Publications and Author of more than twenty-nine books.

NOTE: Mr. Carter passed away before publication of this book, he was a wonderful man and I use his comments with love.

PREFACE

Richard Dreyfus was a neighbor of mine when I lived in Queens. When I left New York for Israel, he had graduated from Julliard School of Music and Drama. Richard went on to make the movie "American Graffiti", and became a star. At that time, his mother was a friend of my mother's. During my travels she kept me informed of his successes in some of her letters to me which I was able to receive at various embassies along my travels, when I was able to pick up my mail. Many years later, I was on assignment for the Miami Herald on their "Nature Island" venue at Disney in Orlando, when we met up again. He wished me luck and said he would have liked to take that trip too! He said he really wants to read my book once I finally publish it! I told him that maybe he could play me in the movie my book should inspire, as we both look so much alike. He laughed that Long Island giddy laugh of his, and said: "Who knows."

My adventures started in 1961. At that time I was a 17-year old teenager living in Queens, New York, after recently moving from Brooklyn. Over a two year period I traveled to Israel, and after seven months in Israel, my African journey began. It started in East Africa and then on to central Africa into the Belgian Congo. Accompanying me to Africa was Eugene Weiss. I met Gene while living, working and studying the Hebrew language at kibbutz Ein Hashofet ("Spring of the judge" as there was a clear year-around spring on the property when founded in 1937) in the more northern part of Israel.

The following are my loved ones who have influenced me to write this book and always encouraged the best in me:

This book is dedicated to my grandfather, David Schwartz. My grandfather had always told me and taught me to enjoy the adventure and learn from the going, as much from getting and the being there. "Papa" David passed away in 1959 when I was almost 13. He missed my Bar Mitzvah by a couple of months and before he died, he made me promise to someday go to Israel and bring back a piece of the land. When I left Israel, I kept some soil to pour on his grave. I named my first son David in his memory. It is also dedicated to all the other wonderful people, and especially my mom Mary, dad Nat, my brother Mike, Aunt Rose and Uncle Bill, my sons David and Brian, also my father-in-law Herb Cooper, and last but never least, my dearest wife Barbara.

Of Special Note* Dr. Gene Weiss, my companion on this odyssey passed away at the age of 72, just before I finally located him to go over old times and for his assistance in the final edit. Gene, more than anyone else is responsible for my life's research on the African portion of this adventure of a life-time. He was a caring and wonderful human being. I am sure he has well established himself with G-d today!

ACKNOWLEDGMENTS

This book, as my nine other labors' of love and often misery, would just not have been possible without the enthusiastic assistance of several people. My friends and acquaintances were excited to be a part of the process of creating this book. First and foremost, and of highly special note in making this book a reality is my wife, Barbara. For half-a-century she has been my most enthusiastic supporter and the one person that has been able to keep me almost out of the procrastinators club. My mother Mary and father Nathan always encouraged me, and also made it possible for me to take my trip of a lifetime. Although mom balked at her 17-year old son leaving the country to live in Israel, with my father's help, she let me out of the coop that was my home in Queens, to pursue my dreams on my own footing. Frankly, everyone I mention in these acknowledgements has definitely helped me make it possible to finally write my true life story of my time in Israel and Africa.

INTRODUCTION

It's been fifty-two years since my journey to Israel and then onto Africa. I have been asked many times, after casually mentioning some of the details of my true-life adventures to friends, family and acquaintances, why I haven't written a book about my life, and my life changing experiences and travels?

More than five decades ago there was no internet, cell phones or social media of any kind. The only way we could communicate with the outside world most of the time, was when we could get a snail-mail out from the embassies that we visited, or lucky enough to find a HAM operator. Some of the letters we sent never reached their intended targets; some took more than a month or even longer to get to mom, Brother Mike, friend Stephanie, etc. As I look back, everything was going at a speed of between 5 to 20 mph. It took us a day, often with an overnight sleeping bag siesta, on rutted, water filled roads (main roads in most cases) decrepit bridges, and nearly mortally relaxed hand-ferry, owner-operators to go just 100-miles. Sometimes it took two days, to even go 40-miles, or we had to make a full backtrack, only to return to our starting place after a full days travel, due to complete bridge washouts over deep ravines and rivers. Most of the time we had to get used to travel as it would have been in America during the time of horse and wagon days. The big difference was that we had 56-British horses pulling us forward.

Over the years I kept the memory of those times of my 18th-19th birthdays, which took place in Israel and Africa. I have written and published some of these memories in many articles about these adventures. Fortunately, I had been able to refer to the diary that I kept along with the photographs that I took during my youthful adventures in both Africa and Asia for this new book. In this book, I've been able to faithfully re-capture my experiences of so long ago, into one publication: this new book about times so long gone by! Thanks to the fact that I carefully archived all my documents, my passport, visas, correspondences and diary I have been able to reconstruct those times and experiences. Over the years, I gave details to family and friends from the countries I had visited and lived in, beside the letters I sent from those countries, and was later able to access the letters and postcards that I sent to them and they saved from so long ago. Because of this, I was able to offer in-depth, the details now published in this book. The letters and diary have helped me greatly to be able to finally publish my new, long overdue book: Africa on a Pin & a Prayer!

The following is a real-life account of our African odyssey, in some cases, into what can be called, prehistoric times. Our adventure of a lifetime changed my teenage life and Gene's, who was more than twenty years old, forever. Gene and I came to Africa, me as a teenager, and Gene as young man and we both became worldlier and grew up quickly in Africa.

After growing up, in an insulated, loving, home, I eventually decided it was time to see the world. At that time, my world and interests consisted of wanting a Corvette (never did get one), late nights and burgers at the diner, rock & roll music, hair sprayed teenyboppers, the movies, fluff talking heads on television, some fishing opportunities sprinkled in on weekends and shopping malls.

From a very early age, my Papa David regaled me with adventures that he had when he was living in Russia. He told me how he had to change his name from Blanc (white) to Schwartz (black) because he had been conscripted into the Cossack's for the Czar and he defected and was forced to change his name, or if caught, he would have been shot. A story that my grandfather told to me has haunted me all these years. He told me how I lost what would have been my aunt. This was based on the fact that she was my papa's sister. One day, my grandfather and aunt took a walk together. She was very young, only a small toddler. They headed out into a field near their cottage and climbed a small hill. According to Papa, suddenly, a giant eagle came from seemingly nowhere, and snatched his sister in its very large and powerful talons. My grandfather tried his best to have the eagle release her, screaming and running along under the big bird, but to no avail, the eagle carried little Chava away, she was never seen again. This incident was as real as the tears in my grandfather's eyes, as he told this story to me! How could anyone forget?

Another story that he told me took place when he was in the Cossacks. He was on his way home with his "Chupka" as he called his horse, during a heavy snow storm (the painting of this incident was in his hallway) when a pack of wolves came in for the kill on his horse. His horse, Chupka kicked one of the wolves, a glancing blow. However, that wolf and the other six other winter hungry carnivores were still after Chupka. My grandfather fired at them with his pistol, but sitting on a jumping, kicking horse did not allow for any decent accuracy with his pistol. Finally, he got lucky and it appeared he hit the Alpha wolf and it took off limping badly, the other wolves then followed. That night he and his horse made it home.

My grandpa had many more stories and he shared them whenever we were together enjoying excellent quality time. When I was very young, as I was told; about two years old, we were at Bungalow Colony for the summer that belonged to one of his cousins in Loch Sheldrake, in upstate New York. It was at a Cuch Alane (cook alone) where there was a central shared kitchen that bungalow renters all used. I remember feeling that it was a true family very warm and loving time. The women were actually enjoying the communal cooking experience and each one was always learning from the other on the right way to do kreplach (a Jewish wonton, oh, so incredibly good) brisket of beef, roast and boiled chicken. I enjoyed the vegetables (even as a little boy), and enjoyed an entire real-life college of bakery product how-to's. One fine sunny early morning, my grandpa David took me fishing with him for the first time! We walked to a lake near the bungalow rental colony, and on the way; he stopped at a large maple tree, he then pulled down a branch which exposed a large leaf. He then held his hand next to the leaf and brought me up close so I could see both his hand and the leaf with the sun shining on and through them. He said: "Do you see these little veins on my hand and on the leaf, both of them were made by the same G-D and they are alike and in so many ways the same." I never forgot that experience, or his words of so long ago, they are so indelibly etched into my memory bank!

So many years later, the first part of my traveling adventure began by ship to Israel. As a teen, I had worked summers in the Catskill Mountains at various tourist hotels. These were the same "Borsht Belt" hotels that contemporaries such as Jerry Lewis, Shecky Green, Phil Silvers, Alan King and a whole host of various comedians from New York and New Jersey, to name a few, were "making their bones." The mostly, Jewish hotels were places like; in Loch Sheldrake, Browns Hotel, The Gradus, Kutshers, the Concord and other hotels in and around Monticello and South Fallsburgh, area of New York. It was at a Glatt Kosher hotel (absolutely kosher) where I met a young Yeshiva student. He talked me into traveling with him to Israel to work on a Kibbutz (communal farm). We were to leave on the ship "Zion" (pronounced Tsion) owned by Israel. This program was underwritten by the Israeli Government to bring young men and women to move to Israel to make Aliyah (going up) "coming home to Israel to become (Olem Chadashim)" new immigrants. "The purpose was to bring youth and introduce new blood to Eretz Yisroel (land of Israel). After the summer jobs in Upstate New York were over, I made an appointment in New York City to visit the offices of the Israeli office responsible for the Aliyah Program. I was asked, actually grilled by two representatives of this ongoing program. Their job was to know why, I, as an American young man would want to go to Israel and my feelings about this potential trip of a lifetime. I answered that as a Jew I felt it necessary to offer my sweat and efforts to assist in making Israel and of course Palestine, which is Israel, green again and pull it back from "desertification. " I ended my interview with the following comment: "I really want to feel the earth of Israel under my fingernails, to touch it, smell it, feel its warmth and invitation to me and the subsequent Jewish people, who will always want to live the thought and reality of someday, living next year in Jerusalem." I guess I said all the right things. But most important I said it and I meant it. They recognized it was no sales pitch and so they accepted me to the program and assigned me to work and study at Kibbutz, Ein Hashofet!

Note* My friend in upstate New York, the one who talked me into going, backed out at the last minute, I went myself, leaving my crying parents sending their child off on the ship, at dockside. My mother Mary told me upon my return, that she never expected to see me again after watching that ship sail away into the Atlantic. She of course prefaced this comment with: "You took 10-years off of my life!" Note* Today, she is alive and well at 94 and still going strong.

CHAPTER ONE

FROM NEW YORK TO KIBBUTZ EIN HASHOFET, ISRAEL

I was amongst many American, Mexican, Canadian, British, French, Iranian, Christian and Jewish teenagers headed for Kibbutz "Ein Hashofet" ("spring of the judge", named after the clear, clean spring on the property) to work and make the land green again. There were about 200 passengers all together on the ship. Because I was aboard the ship to go to Israel to work, my quarters were in steerage with other would-be kibbutzniks for this program. There were eight to a room. That was perfectly OK! Frankly, I didn't spend time in my room except to get about six hours of sleep. The rest of the time I was reading, looking for dolphin and sharks, talking to other ship mates and looking for some serious "tail." I met Edna (the ship Captain's daughter). Edna taught me much about what I could expect living in Israel. Unfortunately, it was just a shipboard romance. She was "killer" gorgeous, her black eyes and sweet, smooth, slightly tan skin and legs fulfilled my teenage fantasies of exotica to the max! Along with all my diverse traveling companions, we were heading there to learn the language and ultimately fit into Israeli society. It was an exciting, youthful adventure for all of us. The adventure for many of us included; eventually becoming inducted into the Israel Defense Forces (that did not come to be for me, because I left for Africa). This was the first time I had been away from my home in the United States and the first time on a ship. The whole new experience was spectacular to me, and certainly very different from what I was used to, or dreamed of before getting on the ship. But on a side note: All the things that I had been taking for granted such as toilet paper, TV, radio, easy access diners and restaurants, malls, were not available once we were on the kibbutz (so you see how much of a spoiled American I was at that time).

After this unbelievable voyage, we finally disembarked at the Port of Haifa. After doing the paper work, getting everything hand-stamped such as entry papers, and inoculation forms, we met up with a bus driver (actually our large van driver) who told us that we could further outfit ourselves just outside the port entrance, with the kinds of clothes and sandals that we would want on the kibbutz. A group of us went into a sandal shop and there we met the proprietor and his wife. They were in their 80's, very friendly and only spoke Yiddish. I saw their identification numbers tattooed on their arms and realized that they were Holocaust survivors. Everyone began trying on hand-made leather sandals. As I was the only one in the group that spoke Yiddish, I asked the owners how much the sandals cost. The old man said: "the sandals are seven grush. At the time it amounted to about a dollar and a quarter. I told the others that were with me the cost of the sandals. The old man then spoke to me in Yiddish. He told me that, being that as a young man I spoke Yiddish, the cost for me would be five grush not seven. I was questioned by the others as to why I could just pay five coins and they have to pay seven for the same sandals. I told them in English that the old man was impressed that I spoke his language. As a special gift to me he gave me a discount. They were not amused! Too bad!

We then boarded the kibbutz van from Haifa and set out for our final destination of the Menashe Hills, where Kibbutz Ein Hashofet was located. During the trip, we passed orange and grapefruit groves, and were told by the driver that we would be working in the groves at Ein Hashofet too! Once we arrived, we were assigned our rooms, and then shown where the toilets were and were asked to assemble in the recreation hall. We were then given the rules, regulations and schedules of how to behave and where everything was on the Kibbutz. We were advised as to when and where our Hebrew classes would take place and the directions to the Beit Ochal (food house) with the times that the meals would be served. They showed us where the used, old newspapers were located for use in the toilets (toilet paper did not exist there). After many letters to my mother, I told her about the lack of toilet paper. She took pity on me and sent me a big box of toilet tissue. I later traded some of the paper for many goodies with my fellow Ulpanists (those that worked for the bed and breakfast and an education in all things Israel, including learning the language at daily classes).

At Nahariya on a Teoul (Trip) I met this gal from Egypt. Her family immigrated to Israel; President Nasser's regime was not friendly to Egypt's Jews. She was a high school senior in the beach side community of Nahariya. She was a sweet, fun-loving girl and we had many fine times together traveling around the country on a few trips to Haifa and Tel Aviv, but mostly to beaches for sun and sand.

Many of my shipmates dropped out of the program due to the generally harsh conditions which were not actually hard at all for those that did not grow up lazy and having a silver spoon permanently lodged in their mouths. Many spoiled and pampered children from the west, who were used to all the available modern conveniences, could not adjust to the reality of where that steak really did come from. Also, how hard it was to work in order to grow food that you need to eat. We were mostly a lazy, spoiled lot. Some got over it and learned (I did) as about half of the 45 mates I arrived with, did too!

I met a wonderful visiting nurse. She was there to meet up with some of her friends on the Kibbutz. When President David Ben Gurion flew to various countries on official business, she was his 20-year old, onboard nurse. She was a Yemenite, Jewish gal with dark silky hair down to the small of her back, with a wit and personality one had to experience, to be believed. I immediately fell in love with a smile and a shrug, her dark eyes and smooth skin and lush natural lips that my lips, only just my cheek, would never experience. She had me enthralled. When she spoke, it was music and poetry to me. To say I was smitten would be an understatement. I thought if we could get married, I would join the IDF and remain in Israel as a new immigrant. This was not to be. She was betrothed to another. I did not have an understanding of the social rules and mores' of the country. It was normal for everyone to hold hands and be warm to each other like sisters and brothers (she did not deceive me on this). I decided it was time to leave Israel via our detour trip to, and sojourn in Africa. (Ultimately, after returning to the United States, I found my beloved 50-years ago, my wife Barbara together now for 47-years). On a trip to visit Ruhama and her family near Tel Aviv, I met her IDF boyfriend. I also was enthralled when her father told me why they had left Yemen to move to Israel. He said in Yemen "Jews could not ride camels"! When I asked him why, he said: "When it comes to Moslems, they would not let anyone who was not a Moslem, to travel with their heads higher than theirs." When we sat at the table eating a delightful and exotic Yemenite dinner and prayed before the meal. I noticed that Ruhama's father swayed back and forth sideways, not in the traditional prayer movements. I was taught from my grandfather and his fellow worshippers that rocking forward and back emphasize the liturgy they read and said. Again I asked him why he swayed sideways. He said: "This is to say to the Arab Moslems; see we ride the camel!" So many things, so many memories of my stay in Israel, this would, I believe take a whole other book to almost include it all.

While in Israel, I lived and worked in various agricultural pursuits and studied the Hebrew language on the Kibbutz (a communal farm environment). Ein Hashofet Kibbutz was settled by two groups of pioneers from Poland and North America in 1937, and named in honor of U.S. Supreme Court Justice Louis D. Brandeis, champion & leader of American Jewry. The kibbutz is located in the biblical hills of Menashe, about 25-miles from the city of Haifa, and about 75-miles north of Tel Aviv. This very rural, tight- knitted community was a wonderful experience for me and as it was also for the other Kibbutzniks. I found that working close to the land of Israel was a blessing in many ways. Just feeling the sweet, good earth on my hands and seeing it under my fingernails, made my heart swell with pride. After two-thousand years, I was touching the face of G-D's country; really G-D's blessing to his peoples and the whole world as well ("Israel, a light unto all the nations"). Today, if you visit, you will fully understand this last statement. There are at least 250-kibbutz's in Israel today, (50-years ago there were more than 500). All the kibbutz's are diverse and extremely interesting communities. Still today, they bring in people from around the world in many different ways. Today, many kibbutzes have "stay and work programs", or motels and hostelries that for a fee, these communities allow visitors to experience the social and working-learning opportunities that each given kibbutz offers. Each kibbutz has its own unique character and special differences in rules, types of amenities and naturally, personality.

The Kibbutz was really a home away from home for me and it was whatever you wanted to make of the experience as well. I wanted a lot, and I gained a lot by working towards and for it!

Four generations live together on the kibbutz. There, they maintain a dynamic, self-contained economic structure and an active social and cultural life. My kibbutz population included approximately

5

800 adults and children, each generation enjoying special benefits provided by the community. The first generations of children are now the leaders of the community, in both economic and social positions, continuing the tradition which had begun by their parents; the founding settlers. Their grandchildren today, fill the children's houses and enjoy a full education, from pre-school through university, along with music, art and athletic enrichment classes. The founding members, who are today over 80-years of age, can choose from a number of suitable work places, activities and health care, all in a quiet and supportive environment.

The way our Ulpan worked was that newbie's (Ulpanists) got up early each day (4-a.m.) except Saturday. They had a breakfast that consisted basically of a hardboiled egg, out- of –the- garden, veggies, Challah bread (a twisted loaf of very favorable and tasty bread) with margarine, plenty of hot or iced tea and my favorite energy confectionary; Halvah. For breakfast it was always family style dining. We then left the "Beit Ochal" eating house; sort of a family style cafeteria. We got on a trailer pulled by a tractor to the fields, or to the orchards and groves. We worked for four hours in irrigation, fruit picking and always watching for vipers that loved the damp area that irrigation created. We then were picked up after work and we headed back to our rooms and bathhouse. After cleaning up, we went to school for Hebrew language classes for about two hours each day. The lunch was the order of the day which included home-made yogurt, fruit and more fresh uncooked veggies. Challah bread and margarine, jelly and more Halvah-oh did I love that fresh vanilla halvah (ever since enjoying that halvah confection, I've sought it out whenever I am in any city that has a Middle Eastern Restaurant). Dinner was a hot veggie plate, a tomato salad, and often, a fish dish.

It wasn't all work and no play on the kibbutz. Time was taken for many recreational pursuits. My favorite had been when the kibbutz regulars took us on "teouls" trips to all parts of Israel, each weekend. We traveled to the Dead Sea and floated high, very high in the super saline, salt in the lowest altitude saltwater body of water in the world.

We covered ourselves with black Dead Sea mud and astringed our bodies and souls. We went to Ein Gedi, which was a beautiful spring and waterfall. We then camped out in sleeping bags. The next day, we swam there in the heat of a September afternoon. We traveled to the northern seaside town of Nahariya, ate falafel and humus and just off the grill, tasty pita bread, with zeiteem (olives) at outdoor kiosks', swam in the Mediterranean and met and made new friends everywhere. Or, we took our own little trips to Tel Aviv, Jerusalem, and Haifa by autobus, or by Citroen auto (one person in our group had this old car).

At the Kibbutz, I am in the center with my arms on one of the Arab carpenters. Samir is 2nd from my left. These were some of my friends from around the world that were on the kibbutz with me in 1961. They were from Australia, Great Britain, Belgium, Iran, Poland, and France to name a few of the countries represented by these Ulpanists.

I had a friend named Samir Gemalich, who lived in Nazareth and worked as a carpenter at the kibbutz. We befriended each other. He had an Indian Motorcycle and took me to his home to meet his family and his twelve sisters. All were a-twitter when I was asked to stay for dinner and sleep over. Samir took me to his home on a Friday night (Saturday was my day off from work and school). Dinner consisted of rice pudding made with goat's milk, containing big raisins and walnuts. Samir's mom milked the goats, crushed the nuts and boiled the rice. It was the very best rice pudding that I ever had then and until now, as well. I noticed that I had the biggest bowl of all, and the girls had little dishes of the terrific pudding. That was all we had for dinner. I felt a bit bad about that, but that's the etiquette in an Arabs home (these were friendly, non-Muslim Arabs, they were Greek Orthodox Christians) and respected my Judaism and were very glad to be living in Israel. Samir's mom told me in the entire Arab world there is no place better for everything, than Israel. She felt like a citizen, (which she was) and was not afraid that anyone would burn down her church or come in the night for her children to rape, pillage and sell them into slavery, calling on Shariya Law as the defacto law of the land. She was a wonderfully hard working woman with a big heart, and Samir and his sisters was a product of this. Samir's father was a shoe maker and made the family living in Jerusalem. He made sandals and shoes and marketed them at the souk (outdoor and indoor market) in Jerusalem. Much of my time off was made on the back of Samir's motorcycle. He loved to ride and visit all of Israel. He was proud of his transportation and stopped all over, to say hello to friends. I enjoyed these stops and remember staying up late at night drinking black mud-like Turkish coffee with enough sugar to make you high if the caffeine didn't. It was enjoyable being with Samir and his friends, who were eager to hear all about the United States and they all wanted to move there, someday. One evening we headed to the movies to see a Russian war movie with Arabic and Hebrew scrolling at the bottom of the screen. I mentioned that I needed to go to the WC bathroom. Samir's friends immediately got up and escorted me there. I told Samir that it was not necessary for his friends to come with me and he said: "Yes it was. Moslems might knife me in there." The ones that I saw coming into the movie theatre did scowl at me, but I was a naïve 17-year old, no matter; I listened to him anyway.

Samir Gemalich (center) and Friends in Nazareth, Israel. They took me everywhere; to the movies, on visits to other friends homes where there was always plenty of dark, black, sugary, Turkish coffee and conversation to go around

.

On the weekends at the farm, sometimes we had chicken, or fish, never beef! Our diets were so fresh vegetable and fruit healthy; I always felt that I could move mountains. At the time, I was 17-years old and quite strong, having been a weight lifting instructor at a Vic Taney Gym, in Manhasset, Long Island, New York for six months. This was prior to coming to Israel and while having to wait for my passport and other travel papers to be completed for this trip. I had graduated from High School when I was 16-years old and had a few part time jobs, (Lender's Bagels sales, fish and appetizer preparer and Assistant Sales Manager for a Super Market, chain store, a life guard and a previously mentioned waiter, etc.) , during the summer, fall and winter of 1960-to early 1961, when I left for Israel.

When I was at the kibbutz, many of the founding fathers and mothers were in their twenties and thirties and driven to keep making a success of their farming community. Today, the culture, economics and society now includes industry as well as agriculture. Some kibbutz members now also work outside the community to provide income. Many are musicians, artists, authors, professors and sculptures' living in a unique creative atmosphere, which also offers free time for hobbies and study for personal advancement. The kibbutz agricultural branches included poultry, dairy and beef cattle, field crops and avocado orchards and groves of citrus. When I was there, I worked in many of their early agricultural projects, including picking up rocks to make fallow fields ready for planting the orchards, citrus groves, irrigation systems for their apple and citrus trees of today and generally learning the ropes of what a farmer is all about-good hard, but smart work on and with the land-a partnership if you will, with nature. Learning to sow before the reaping and reaping effectively and righteously. Recently, (39-years later), I visited Kibbutz Ein Hashofet during a research trip for a new book and for magazine articles. I was amazed at their new industrial projects in automotive equipment and high-tech lighting systems. I felt at home immediately and was made to feel that way by members who welcomed me warmly and wonderfully. I attempted to visit my Hebrew language teacher, Sarah. Sarah was a European concentration camp survivor, whom I loved as a great mentor and fine linguist: Sarah spoke Hebrew, Arabic, Russian, Polish, Serbian, Ukrainian and other dialects and languages. She was a most fascinating and unique human being, who the Nazi's put through hell and back! Doctor Mengele, used her in an experiment. The good doctor grafted a goat's leg, after amputating her good leg for experimentation purposes. If Sarah had not been freed by the allies soon after her horrible operation from this horrendous German Nazi experiment, she would have died from infections. She immigrated to Israel in 1947. One rainy day, she told our class the real story of the Exodus! I think of her each time I think of Israel, which is every day! As this book has come to final publishing, she too has continued her journey into the next world and hopefully to her next chapter-a place and page we all must turn someday!

I had met Dr. Gene Weiss at the kibbutz in early 1962. At that time he was a public health major at Berkeley College in California. Gene had come from Scotland, where he attended Edinburgh University for his Masters Degree. The Ford Foundation had agreed to underwrite dollars for Gene to study African diseases on a tour throughout the continent. We became fast friends. My outgoing personality and knowledge of a few languages such as German, Hebrew, and Spanish was what Gene needed to assist with his journey to Africa. I even studied Swahili and was able to learn the basics before we even departed for East Africa. My fondness of the martial arts and my strong eye-to-hand coordination, allowed me to be able to accurately throw knives and hatchets at targets. It did not go unnoticed by Gene, he later told me that prior to inviting me along on the expedition he had witnessed my demonstrations of knife and hatchet throwing. He also saw the rapport that I had with some of the Christian Arab carpenters from Nazareth that worked as part-time contractors on the Kibbutz. He felt I was outgoing and made friends easily. He told me of this much later on in our trip together. Gene was studious, less impulsive and more introversive than I was, and thus he felt we would make good traveling companions. Gene believed that we were heading to a land that would need both our strengths and talents. He was about four years older than me, spoke French and in the Congo, that would prove to be of utmost importance. French was the second language of the country (a first language, especially in the larger cities). This was because of the long standing Belgian influence in the African nation and also the French Missionaries who taught their Christian religion in French. The local language was Lingalese and I never did learn that language, but I did learn quite a bit of French. Speaking French, allowed me to get along in the Congo.

Gene (Right) and I, as we headed across another African river by ferry, I always trolled for predator fish such as Tigerfish and Wolfish, during the crossings.

CHAPTER TWO

ISRAEL AND TRAVEL BY BOAT TO AFRICA

Being an impulsive teenager, when Gene Weiss asked me if I would like to join him on his trip to Africa, I jumped at the chance. My six-month stay on the Kibbutz was nearly up and after finding that the girl I loved (a Yemenite Jewish gal who was already engaged to an Air Force Pilot), I had little to hold me in Israel at that time. My plan was to go to France with Marcel, a Parisian gal that I had met. We became fast friends at the kibbutz communal farm. Marcel had plans for me in a very personal way; I did not match her enthusiasm for those plans! I did want to stay friends and visit Paris. However, all my plans changed when Gene told me of the excellent fishing opportunities that I would find in Africa. I was, and have always been a sucker for a good fishing trip!

Why visit Africa?

Well, after visiting one of the smallest and most vibrant of nations in the world; Israel, Africa with all of its unique countries and the world's second-largest and second-most-populous continent, seemed like a great place to continue my journeys. The approximately, 12 million square miles, which includes some island communities, accounts for and covers six percent of the Earth's total surface area and also about 20 percent of the total land area, had my imagination working overtime. Living on this continent with the moniker: "The Dark Continent" has more than 1.0 billion people going about their business and lives there. Africa has about 15% of the world's population. The continent is surrounded by the Indian Ocean, the Atlantic Ocean, the Mediterranean Sea to the north, and the Suez Canal. Madagascar and various archipelagoes also make up part of Africa.

Africa is the youngest continent in terms of the ages of its population. 50-percent of Africans are 19 years old or younger. In Africa, people for the most part, do not have longevity as a strong suite compared to most of the rest of the world's populations. The many reasons for this are inadequate early and life diet and so many different diseases that are endemic to Africa. Also, health care is mainly a hit or miss luxury for Africans, but in more recent times there has been some help coming in from what I like to call; "the outside world!"

"Africa's name is derived from an ancient area in modern day Tunisia known as Ifriqiya or sunny place, in Tamazight." The Brits had a hard time pronouncing it, so today we have Africa. As an adventurous youth, Africa would naturally be my first major travel choice, as I know now at this point of my life, that it would take many lifetimes to discover the mysteries that all of Africa presents to those that seek this knowledge and adventure. Wikipedia information-October-2013

In preparation for our journey, we had to get clearance from the Embassies of the African countries that we hoped to visit. This was no easy task, as in those days as probably it is today too. Each and every African Embassy had their own rationale for approving visas and they had to be worked with on an individual basis. Fortunately, some Embassies were cooperative, however some were not. We were persistent, and in a few weeks, we had all our visas!

The countries we planned to visit for the first year of our adventure was Zanzibar, Tanganyika (now called Tanzania), Ethiopia, Somalia, Kenya, Uganda, Rwanda, Burundi and then head into the Congo. It came to pass that we eventually did visit all the above.

While waiting for our papers, visas and appointments for inoculations, I attended psychology classes (in the Hebrew language) at Jerusalem University, spent time with friends and their families that I met at the Kibbutz and who I also considered were my family in Jerusalem. That's the way it was in Israel at that time (hopefully still is for most Israelis) you really felt at home there. My extra time was spent trying to learn all I could about the countries that I was about to embark to.

Reuben, my friend on Kibbutz Ein Hashofet came from Romania. He and his father invited me to live with them while in Jerusalem and I learned of their plight. The Romanian Communists threw them off of their farm. It was their homestead for many generations of their family. The Communists forced them to move and Israel helped and made it easy for them to emigrate as Oalim Chadashim (new immigrants). Rueben's father lived in a dingy flat, and he lamented to me how his way of life and livelihood as a farmer was taken away from him in Romania. It had been his life and heritage. It was in Romania, where he enjoyed his family, neighbors and his land and agricultural business. He told me he just could not get over being robbed of his home and livelihood. He had been a farmer all his life; he later committed suicide, a few months after I had left for Africa. I found out about this tragedy many months later. The sadness that I saw and felt in that flat was so palpable that today, some 52-years later; I can still feel that sadness when I think of Reuben and his poor father. Hopefully, Rueben has, and is having a fruitful and happy life in Israel.

The Western Wall in Jerusalem. Down through the 2000 year history of the Jews being dispersed around the world; one call by Jews is part of each prayer about their homeland is: "Next Year in Jerusalem." The Wall is the remnant of the Jewish Temple destroyed by the Romans 2000 years ago. Until 1967, Jews could not come here to pray. Jordanian Moslems were in control of Jerusalem with their gold domed Al Aqsa Mosque built directly over the "bones" of the Jewish Temple in Old Jerusalem. As they made war on Israel on Yom Kippur; the holiest day of the year, Arabs lost the city back to the original biblical inhabitants-The Jewish People! It took 2000 years and now once again; all of Jerusalem is accessible as the capital of Israel.

It took nearly a month to get all of our visas and necessary papers in Jerusalem and Tel Aviv. After booking passage on the very last sailing of the "Pidawnyunt", we embarked on our journey after paying $50-dollars each for our week-long passage. The Pidawnyunt was a New Delhi, Indian cruising freighter that also had provisions for taking fifty paying passengers, most of whom were traveling to South Africa. To get to the ship, we had flown to Eilat which is located in the southernmost part of Israel from Tel Aviv. The ship sailed from the Gulf of Aqaba, 180 kilometers to the Indian Ocean, through and from the Red Sea. Eilat, 52-years ago was a sparsely populated and mainly undeveloped, rather sleepy, fishing, waterfront town. Today, Eilat is an internationally known tourism Mecca that has spectacular Red Sea attractions, overlooking clear, clean reef-filled waters, world-class cuisine, great mineral, precious gems and gift shops and numerous cultural events. Today, accommodations in Eilat are priced for bearers of plastic, leather wallets, and fine pocket books. However, the average Israeli and visitor can easily visit Eilat on a budget basis, as well. You may ask how I know things based on modern times in Israel and the answer is: that since 1961, I've taken one or more extended trips to Israel each decade, since that time.

The Pidawnyunt; the New Delhi freighter that carried us to Tanganyika. It had passenger space for 50 and stopped in several countries off loading agricultural goods and us, from Israel.

On our trip to Africa, we made many new acquaintances on this ship and witnessed some amazing things on the Indian Ocean. Unfamiliar places make common bed-fellows of sometimes, very uncommon people. The joy of sharing in these experiences is done for very simple reasons: The first being uncertainty, the second anxiety that uncertainty can cause, the third is that the new smells, exotic aroma essences and sights are not as enjoyable without peer reinforcement for young and old. Sharing and companionship doubles the pleasure and the taste of traveling to faraway places. You can only talk to yourself for so long before realizing you are only preaching to your own singularly, personal choir. Collating, processing and feeling the experiences of a lifetime by a boy not quite 18 years old, was and still would be a difficult and lonely undertaking if done alone.

After waking on the third day at sea, I bounded out of my bunk bed, eager for another day of adventure. I went to the dining room and enjoyed an English style breakfast of scones, tea with lemon, crumpets and blackberry jam. I came up from the dining room and walked to the stern of the ship. Actually, I did this every morning of our two weeks on the water, in hopes of watching the fabulous striped and spinner dolphins cavorting in the wake and alongside the freighter. Most of the rest of the time at sea, I read Tolstoy's War & Peace and started all the longer novels I never had time to start before, let alone, finish, before having so much reading time at sea.

On a particularly clear and bright morning, I watched as the galley crew threw large black plastic bags of garbage overboard, as they did daily (No laws in effect in those days governing ocean dumping). This day however, at least for me was very different. As I watched the bags hit the water and ride high and dry in the bubbled and white wake of the ships propeller wash; I spotted a very large creature. I thought it was a shark which came up and opened a cavernous mouth and seem to inhale one of these large, oversize plastic bags in one boiling swallow. Excited and amazed, I was totally overwhelmed with the scene I had just witnessed. I strained my eyes to see if more of the bags would disappear and again, another bag went under in a white boil of water that resembled a small whirlpool. I raced up to the bridge to ask the Captains opinion of what these great creatures were and after describing the scene to the captain, he gave me this cryptic answer: "My boy, no one knows what incredible fish and creatures live in these waters of the Indian Ocean. There are creatures here that boggle the imagination with their size and diversity". Well, you can imagine the impression this made on a youth that had an imagination as large as the ocean he traveled on. I was 17-years old and never forgot that experience and still today wonder what those great fish were.

We landed to off-load Jaffa oranges from Israel in the Port of Massawa in Ethiopia and watched the antique and overloaded steam train that ferried the cargo to awaiting trucks, strain under the load. The front wheels of this antique contraption lifted up and off the tracks, and made the entire scene reminiscent of a Keystone Cops comedy piece and a Toonerville Trolley skit, all rolled into one. Thousands of oranges ended up in the oil slick that was the harbor, from the inept, overly casual way they were off-loaded. No one seemed to mind, and for the ships hands, who leaned over the railing and bemusedly watched and chattered from the ship, it seemed that this was a rather common occurrence for them.

My new found shipmates encouraged us to visit the surrounding town of Massawa, Eritrea. Massawa, a port town that had gold temple roofs shining in the sun, from Emperor Hailie Selasie's time and filthy black streets that smelled of urine, decay, debauchery and disease.

Massawa, "filthy" Massawa was my first experience with the degradation of children selling themselves as sexual objects. Little blue-eyed boys and girls propositioned us. These chocolate skinned children, we were to learn, were the progeny of the many Italians that were stationed and had strong economic control of Ethiopia and Eritrea for a very long time. There were hundreds of these bedraggled and waifish young people, who, for a bit of food would do anything, and whose degradation was directly proportional it seemed to their miserable predicament. What I saw there were small, dilapidated attached homes; they were once clean and attractive abodes, now remnants of foreign occupational Italian provincial, vacated by the victors. They stood dirty and run-down in so many more ways than architecturally. These homes had young girls hanging out of every window, sitting on the front steps leading to their front doors, vying for the attention of anyone they could get to pay them a few cents for their sexual favors'.

Many of these girls and young boys were also the orphans of the lonely loins of sailors and occupiers alike, who made babies by the thousands. They had no intention or thought of caring for these children that came into the world, in most cases, long after they returned to their homelands. These were children out of sight and of course out of mind to the so-called authorities, who were all pulling for no one else, but their own bribes they could collect. Like many politicians and so-called, public servants everywhere. The sailors left for their homes across the world. The Italians went home to "Das Boot" and should have felt it on the posterior too. My idealistic and youthful mind could not fully understand how these children, who hostage their body for food and the right to survive, actually survived to anything resembling old age. I could not comprehend the dilemma of these abused babies. A few of the shipboard travelers availed themselves of these children's sexual favors. I could not talk to them, nor look at them again for the rest of the time that I was aboard ship. I could not even take a photo of those children on that street of oblivion, whose images still haunt me when I think of that experience. I returned to the ship disgusted. It, for me was the saddest sight of the entire trip to Africa and remains today, a vivid remembrance of the worst in man. The local governments made little or no attempt to care for these children, who were left to starve and fend for themselves, in the hell-hole that was Massawa, Ethiopia.

We later re-boarded our ship and headed for Djibouti, Somalia. I recall it being so incredibly hot in Somalia, that I was forced to put my shirt around my head for protection. I soon understood why the Arabs that I saw everywhere wore the headgear and robes they are known for. They needed to shade themselves from the 110-degree heat. I had to breathe through my mouth, because the air was too hot for my sinuses and nearly caused me to black out. Thus, my nose wasn't much good for anything except to exhale, not breathe through.

This mosque in Somalia is where it was against Moslems protocol to take a picture of them. They were afraid you'd capture their souls and harm them. It's from Djibouti Somalia, where today, pirates sally forth to hostage boating traffic on the Indian Ocean.

Foolishly, near a picturesque, pointy roofed Moslem mosque, I aimed my camera at a throng of people milling around the entrance. I then was immediately chased by a club and sword-wielding horde. They all had one thing in common; they wanted my blood. I found out fast from a policeman who was directing traffic and who I nearly clung to. He advised me that the crowd had to see me destroy the film and then I would be able to go away unharmed. Otherwise, he would have to jail me for my own protection. I took the film out of the camera quickly and allowed the shrieking mob to step on the film and destroy it. Only then did the mob retreat. Immediately I made plans to return to the boat. Quickly I took some shots from the hip, so I was not seen aiming the camera at anyone or anything in particular. These Muslim were backward people that believed that I had captured their souls with my camera and could cause them harm if I wanted to, with their image in my possession. That experience as I recall, reminded me of Haiti and the voodoo weirdness. After all, the mind is hostage to the truth and to the lie as well! Mix in millenniums' of superstition and the surreal becomes reality to those that cannot think for themselves. If that had happened in these times, I surely would have had my throat slit in that filthy miasma, of what the Middle Ages must have been like!

On the way back to my ship, I saw a freighter in the harbor filled with camels covering the entire front half of that ship. I took a picture of this, but it didn't survive the trip, I lost a couple of film rolls to an accident when we were in the Congo, fortunately most of my film did survive to ultimately be processed, some of which is now seen in this book.

A ship load of camels at the port in Djibouti, Somalia, as it was heading for Egypt. That ship and the surrounding area really smelled from all the camel dung and sweat in the over 110+-degree heat.

The freighters itinerary called for cruising out of the Red Sea, past the Suez, and the Gaza strip; around the ancient and biblically known Cape Guard-A-Fui (fire guard), known once for an ancient giant bonfire that once kept sailing ships of the past away from the rocky reefs of the North-eastern African Continent. We were scheduled to stop in Ethiopia, Somalia, Kenya and Tanganyika. The ship would drop us in Dar es Salaam, (Port of Peace) Tanganyika and head on to South Africa.

As I explained, I had returned to the ship in disgust that day in Massawa. That night, I lay awake thinking of my luck having been born into a world of loving, real parents and relatives. I cried myself to sleep over one of the first, real worldly shocks of my life. I awoke to sun and brisk winds which buffeted my face with the smell and feel of clean and crisp, salt air. After breakfast and some research in the ships library of what we can expect in Tanganyika from a travel book that I found there, I again went topside and peered across the Indian Oceans horizon. I leaned on the ships railing and day-dreamed about what it would be like to travel across the entire African continent. I pictured huge tiger fish and catfish the size of Volkswagens, pulling my dugout canoe around a wild jungle, Tropical River. I dreamed of animals that were out in the open, real and untamed. I dreamed of peoples from their cultural heritages, doing things the way they were done before there were history books. I had already experienced sights, sounds and aromas that were highly exotic to a boy from Brooklyn. The only exotic things I remembered from Brooklyn, was a Hebrew National hot dog loaded with sauerkraut and Nathans excellent French fries, tomato catsup at the ready! I still think that was the best of Brooklyn I personally experienced. When I was twelve years old I met a young girl named Ronnie. She was my first girlfriend. We were in a bungalow colony in South Fallsburgh, New York and kissed frequently under a lone apple tree on a hill overlooking the colony. We vowed that when we got home to the big city we'd see each other again and maybe get married someday. We did see each other again! I went to Coney Island thanks to my father driving me there and we had Nathans hot dogs and said goodbye to each other. Her parents felt that I was not ever going to be a millionaire, so they had their daughter, Ronnie break it off. We were twelve; it was the best and worst hot dog memory of my life! But, I still liked sauerkraut and found a new love too; women!

CHAPTER THREE

TANGANYIKA TO ZANZIBAR, GARLIC AND ON TO KENYA AND UGANDA

The sun was setting over a red sky when we arrived in the port city of Dar Es Salaam; Tanganyika (today called Tanzania, incorporating the Island of Zanzibar with Tanganyika and being harmed by the Muslim fanatics that have of late been burning Catholic Churches). This was the last port of call from the ship, before it headed to South Africa. This was our debarkation point from the Pidawnyunt ship. We quickly found a hotel, and soon met a few British officers, looking spiffy in their uniforms and who were stationed at a base in Dar es Salaam. They were curious about our trip and invited us for some smoked sausage & pints.

In those days, the British soldiers lived in barracks in an incredibly beautiful port city. When the sun set over Dar Es Salem (Port Of Peace) Bay, the colors were breathtaking; golden hued, with red and yellowish streaks of fiery-finger-like ribbons painting the exotic sky. The "Brits" informed us, after asking us what we planned to do in Africa, that we were foolhardy to try to cross Africa because of the political and social unrest that we were later to find in almost all of the nations that we visited. Africa was then, and is today constantly in turmoil due mostly to the Jihad that is ongoing from the radical Islamists Muslims on that still "Dark Continent." The tribal conflicts and continual sectarian rivalries too, continuously add to the dysfunction of this vast black and still verdantly green continent. More than fifty years later, since our visit, it seems nothing has really changed. In fact, I believe it's gotten worse in a few of the nations that we visited. During the time after we left, there was a legacy of Idi Amin the "butcher" in Uganda, and the major genocide of the Rwandans and only G-D knows how many Congolese have perished and still are!

A BIT OF TANGANYIKA HISTORY

There is evidence that people from the Sudan and Ethiopia border areas moved to what is today called Tanzania, sometime about 3000 years ago, or a bit later on. The Masai represent a more recent migration from present day South Sudan within the past 1,600 to 450 years. Bantu peoples also moved into the Lake Tanganyika/ Lake Victoria areas called the "lake regions." These peoples had and brought with them the West African planting tradition. A major staple agricultural product came with them, this product is yams.

"The people of Tanzania have been associated with the production of steel. The Haya people on the western shores of Lake Victoria invented a type of high-heat blast furnace that allowed them to forge carbon steel at temperatures exceeding 1,820 °C (3,310 °F) more than 1,500 years ago.

Travelers and merchants from the Persian Gulf and western India have visited the East African coast since early in the first millennium AD. Islam was practiced on the Swahili Coast as early as the eighth or ninth century AD. According to Timothy Insoll, "Figures record the exporting of 718,000 slaves from the Swahili coast during the 19th century, and the retention of 769,000 on the coast." I am always amazed when so many African Americans seem to blame everyone else besides the Muslims, for their forefather's enslavements.

Fat oil salesman sell strips of animal fat to be rendered into cooking oil by local women preparing to cook meals for their families.

In the late 19th century, Imperial Germany conquered the regions that are now Tanzania (minus Zanzibar) and incorporated them into German East Africa. The post–World War I accords and the League of Nations charter designated the area a British Mandate, except for the Kionga Triangle, a small area in the southeast that was incorporated into Portuguese East Africa (later Mozambique).

British rule came to an end in 1961 after a relatively peaceful (compared with neighboring Kenya, for instance) transition to independence. In 1954, Julius Nyerere transformed an organization into the politically oriented Tanganyika African National Union (TANU). TANU's main objective was to achieve national sovereignty for Tanganyika. A campaign to register new members was launched, and within a year TANU had become the leading political organization in the country. " Wikipedia information-October-2013

Nyerere became Minister of British-administered Tanganyika in 1960 and continued as Prime Minister when Tanganyika became independent in 1961. We visited and met one of his Ministers to talk about health issues that Gene wanted to document.

In 1967, Nyerere's first presidency took a turn to the left after the Arusha Declaration, which codified a commitment to socialism in Pan-

African fashion. After the declaration, banks and many large industries were nationalized.

After the Zanzibar Revolution overthrew the Arab dynasty in neighboring Zanzibar, which had become independent in 1963, the archipelago merged with mainland Tanganyika on 26 April 1964. The union of the two, hitherto separate, regions was controversial among many of Zanzibar's locals (even those sympathetic to the revolution) but was accepted by both the Nyerere government and the Revolutionary Government of Zanzibar owing to shared political values and goals.

"From the late 1970s, Tanzania's economy took a turn for the worse. Tanzania was also aligned with China, which from 1970 to 1975 financed and helped build the 1,160 mile long TAZARA Railway from Dar es Salaam Port, to Zambia. Today, the economy is heavily based on agriculture, which accounts for more than 25 percent of gross domestic product, provides 85 percent of exports, and employs 80 percent of the workforce. The religious makeup of Tanzania today is: Islam about 40%, Christianity around 40%, Animism about 20% and approximately 5% various other religions such as Buddhists, Hindus, and Bahá'ís

Currently being exploited in Tanzania are vast amounts of minerals including gold, diamonds, coal, iron, uranium, nickel, chromium, tin, platinum, coltan, niobium, natural gas, and others. The country is also known for Tanzanite, a type of precious gemstone that is found only in Tanzania.

In 2011, Tanzania was the fifteenth-largest producer of gold in the world and the third-largest in Africa after South Africa and Ghana and just ahead of Mali. The value of the gold produced in Tanzania in 2011 was over US $2.5 billion, representing 10.5 percent of the country's gross domestic product." Wikipedia information-October-2013

You can be assured this gold wealth, the highest ounce price in history, very little if any ever trickled down to the poor and needy in this country rife with "baksheesh" (bribery payoffs). Child labor is common in Tanzania with millions of children working. It is more common with girls rather than boys. Girls are commonly employed as domestic servants, sometimes by force. Poor children in particular are trafficked internally for commercial sexual exploitation. Again, in the

52-years since being in Tanganyika nothing much has changed, actually, I believe things have gotten worse.

"At 365,800 square miles, Tanzania is the world's 31st-largest country and the 13th largest in Africa. Tanzania is mountainous in the northeast, where Mount Kilimanjaro, Africa's highest peak, is situated. Three of Africa's Great Lakes are partly within Tanzania. To the north and west lie Lake Victoria, Africa's largest lake, and Lake Tanganyika, the continent's deepest lake, known for its unique species of fish. To the southwest lies Lake Nyasa. Central Tanzania is a large plateau, with plains and arable land. The eastern shore is hot and humid, with the Zanzibar Archipelago just offshore.

Tanzania contains many large and ecologically significant wildlife parks and reserves, including the Ngorongoro Conservation Area, Tarangire National Park, Lake Manyara National Park, and the Serengeti National Park in the north and the Selous Game Reserve, Ruaha National Park, and Mikumi National Park in the south. Gombe Stream National Park in the west is known as the site of Dr. Jane Goodall's studies of chimpanzee behavior." Wikipedia information-October-2013

The government of Tanzania through its department of tourism is working on a campaign to promote the Kalambo water falls in the southwestern region of Rukwa as one of Tanzania's main tourist destinations. The Kalambo Falls are the second highest in Africa and are located near the southern tip of Lake Tanganyika. The Menai Bay Conservation Area is Zanzibar's largest marine protected area. We never did see these falls and wished we had. Tanzania has considerable wildlife habitat, including much of the Serengeti Plain, where the white-bearded wildebeest and other antelope types, participate in a large-scale annual migration. Up to 250,000 wildebeest perish each year in the long and arduous movement to find forage in the dry season. Tanzania is also home to 130 amphibian and over 275 reptile species.

One of Tanzania's and other parts of eastern Africa's, most common cultural dishes is Ugali. It is mainly composed of corn and is similar to the consistency of porridge, giving it its second name of corn meal porridge. We did eat this dish and it would have gone well with a main dish of meatloaf and mashed potatoes, Ugali is much like creamed corn out of a can.

Swahili and English are the official languages; however the former is the national language. English is still the language of higher courts, it can however be considered a de facto official language. There are over 100 different (tribal) languages spoken in Tanzania, including Masai, Sukuma and Makonde. The first language typically learned by a Tanzanian is that of his or her ethnic group, with Swahili and English learned thereafter

As I was interested in learning languages and recognizing that speaking the language of the country's that we visited would be the most advantageous way to travel and live in that country. I worked at learning Swahili on the "go." Just in this one country of Tanzania there are so many languages and when you add in all the other countries (Congo has more than 500 different languages besides French and Lingalese) you realize that the historical story about how G-D confounded the people of Babel. They couldn't understand each other, so killed each other off with no normal communication of how to work things out amicably). I call it the Tower of Babel syndrome (as in the modern word Babel means mumbling incoherent words with no mutual understanding). This does not make for a great peace between nations and their peoples (sort of what's happening in our American Government now). A huge result of this in history and today is; things stay the way they were-no easy transfer of ideas and growth in all areas of people lives. There is no networking going on in much of Africa, so the past stays in the past! So, even before we hit the shores of Dar Es Salam Port of Peace, Tanganyika, I had been reading and studying Swahili. By the time I left East Africa for the Congo, (as I said "on the go,") I was able to speak and understand the language enough to get along very well. I was actually interpreting for Gene when asking for directions, or just about anything we wanted to know about.

Gene and I were young and we both in a varying degree, felt quite omnipotent at the time. We were also imbued with a youthful exuberance that also translated itself into a strong case of idealism, foolhardiness and taking chances we wouldn't have, if we were more mature and worldly. We were going to make everyone's lives brighter and better because we were Americans. As Americans, we cared for the people, flora and fauna of this great cradle of creation.

Giraffe- The longest neck of any animal in the world; they have a very funny personality. I was relaxing with my back to a tire on the Land Rover in the Karamojan Desert and this relatively young giraffe's curiosity almost got the better of her-yes I took inventory as it sauntered away after I clicked the Brownie

Oh, how foolish we were--but only to the extent that we did not fear for our lives and had the naiveté of babes in the woods. We believed that we could make a difference for the better, in the lives that inhabited this continent.

It was in Tanganyika where we met Hans Gerlinger. Hans was a former French paroled German Nazi concentration camp guard. We met him quite by accident. His plans were to travel to Zanzibar during the same time period that we were. It was Gerlinger who taught us the value of all things garlic.

He was on his way to the Seychelles Islands from Zanzibar. He heard rumors that the women out-numbered men on these islands ten to one. Additionally, the women were beautiful! Hans had been locked up in a French prison for all the years since the Second World War and was looking to make up for lost time on the dating scene. I speak Yiddish, a very close cousin linguistically to German, so Hans and I were able to communicate very well. Gerlinger could not understand how I spoke a language so close to German so well. He said, "being a young American," and when I told him that Gene and I were Jewish and I had learned Yiddish from my grandparents, who thankfully had not been burned up in Germany, he cried and asked us for forgiveness. I also told him very directly that the Yiddish language was not dead. Whole cities in the USA had many Jewish people who spoke it and we had newspapers that printed it. I went into the fact that Klezmer music was popular not only with Jews, but people of all nationalities that loved good, vibrant music. He told us how he had been in hell during the war and ever since too. His conversations included many details that I have since tried to forget. He didn't give us the whole picture; mind you, just the particulars too painful to bear thinking about and too horrible for me to print. Frankly, I didn't believe he was truly sorry; he had lived it like almost all Germans at that time. After all, they voted Hitler in, supported his fascism and believed the lies that their scapegoats had to live and die in a most hellish way with. But, somehow I liked this guy anyway! After-all, I was young and trusting-I wanted to learn and experience everything, no matter what or when it did, or was to occur.

Gerlinger asked us if he might travel with us to the clove "spice" island of Zanzibar. We were glad to have him as a traveling companion. He seemed to know the "ropes," having already extensively traveled through Africa and the Congo on his own and was twice our age. I credit him for probably saving our lives with the advice he gave us and for the most part we heeded, as we later traveled through the Central part of the African continent, as well.

He told us of things such as using garlic extensively to ward off internal and external parasites and bugs. He warned us not to deal in contraband diamonds or gemstones (which later tempted us and could have been our downfall, had we not been so soundly warned by Hans and later others, of our possible execution if we dealt in diamonds without proper papers). If not for Hans, we might have become hopelessly ill, or died from diseases brought on by insect pests that were rampant in Africa. Had he not made a point to soundly instill some fear of these dangers and how to prevent them, we probably would have had serious repercussions for our safety and health.

Me and Hans Gerlinger—Hans was a good traveling companion to Zanzibar. He also taught us about all things garlic and allowed me to practice my German and Yiddish.

Since my travels to Africa, I learned quite a bit about the history and value of garlic. Garlic (Allium sativum) is an herb, which for thousands of years has been an important health food. In Egypt, garlic helped build the pyramids due to laborers' were being fed this wonderful "stink bulb" for it's strengthening of these workers and offering them resistance to waterborne diseases. Garlic was found in the tombs of Pharaohs'. Ancient Greeks and other warrior groups such as the Roman Legions ate garlic for courage and strength. Athletes in the early Greek Olympic Games chewed garlic to give them energetic endurance and lovers ate it to give them sexual endurance as well. Romans used crushed garlic as poultices for wounds and it was written in ancient archives, that it was used to cure hemorrhoids. Today, at my farm I grow and use garlic in most of our dishes. I have not had a cold in the six years. I have used garlic at the farm for many purposes, nor have anyone I share my garlic with have had any flu issues. Why does garlic stink? Sulphur compounds in garlic make this bulb smell. Much of the smell comes from the yellowish garlic oil. The garlic smell is excreted through the lungs and skin. So when we sweated in our tropical environs, we had a nearly armor coat of protection from a wide variety of insects and also various internal parasites. Recalling the one important medical breakthrough for wounded military troops was sulphur. Sulphur was applied to wounds to stave off and also deal with topical infections from bullet, shrapnel and other wounds and scratches. There are numerous varieties of Allium sativum (cloved garlic) and they all have sulphur compounds in their oils. In Africa there truly are vampires, not the kinds where people turn into vampire bats, but the biting and stinging, leaching and yes, vampire bats too! In historic times, people did wear garlic around their necks. They believed that this would ward off vampires, and give you the strength of garlic without the odor that goes with eating it. OK! I've been eating garlic all my life and I personally have never been attacked by a vampire, just leeches that live in banks and credit bureaus. If I was late with a payment by more than one week, some of them have attempted to attach themselves to me! Rest assured, they always failed!

Heading on to Zanzibar's soft, spicy clove fragrances that were able to be experienced well before the island came into sight. The wafting aroma of cloves was a pleasant and exotic introduction, especially given the fact that we were on a dhow (nasty, wind powered filthy, Indian, Arab, inter-island transport), and that meant the clove aroma did not have to compete with the exhaust of the engine, just urine and rotten fish smells. There was no engine. What we made up for in lack of noise was made up in the filth and water bugs that crawled on us, as we lay on the deck in our sleeping bags overnight.

The privy on our transport was a hole in the stern of the vessel with a hand washing, water bucket to clean yourself with, minus any type of towels. To say that conditions were primitive would be a major understatement. It was an experience (as many are in our lives) that at the time, was very unpleasant, but lives like many of these moments that pass so quickly through our youth; indelibly! Today, the thoughts about these distant memories can't help but bring a curl of a smile to my lips in their remembrances. As a side note on privies and the cleaning of oneself after using these primitive privies, protocol is that you do not offer the hand that does the cleaning of oneself in a handshake (the left hand usually) as it is uncouth to an Arab. Also, when we were in East Africa, we never found toilet paper anywhere except in the best hotels. So we visited these hotels when we needed to use the privies, when in those cities. We never drank directly out of a glass, always through a straw; as they just could not sanitize anything due to lack of hot enough water to do so. So we learned not to touch our lips to glass or plastics-we used straws! Whatever we ate, we made sure it all started out very hot, both in temperature degrees and spices. No matter what, or where we slept, we always checked our clothes and shoes carefully; to be sure there were no insects, snakes, etc. to sting or bite us. It was a good move on our part; as on one occasion, one of my shoes became a haven for a Recluse spider. It would probably have killed me out there in the veldt, far away from any medical assistance. We had no communications available in those days. There were no cell phones, telephones, just jungle drums and runners. Some towns had telegraph equipment and some that did, lost it intermittently due to wires being stolen for jewelry-virtually everywhere we went we saw women wearing the telegraph wires.

Copper wires in their ears and around their necks. The only gold we saw was around the necks of chiefs and some of their numerous brides. Everyone else had stolen copper wire for their jewelry and pretty rocks with holes in them strung through, with elephant hair or woven vine, ties.

As we arrived at the dock area in Zanzibar, young boys dove into the crystal clear waters next to the dhow. They dove for coins thrown into the water by tourists. The tourists came by the wharf to look at the boats and just gawk at the workers that were muscled and gleaming, wet from the perspiration from the backbreaking work of loading and unloading tons of goods and supplies from mainland Africa.

After being covered up overnight on that dhow by roaches, and various water-bugs, Gene and I could not wait to find a hotel and take a bath. We heard that the Pigale' Hotel had good food and the elderly French proprietress was very friendly and, as it turned out, she was to be very helpful during our two week visit to Zanzibar. We were not disappointed!

Francine was a fabulous hostess and must have been a beautiful redhead in her youth. She had charmed the service personnel of the

Second World War stationed at the air base. This base is now a missile base that was an active place as late as 1963 and still is today.

Young boys diving for coins that the tourists tossed into the crystal clear waters of the port docks of Zanzibar in 1963.

We began eating garlic the morning of our arrival and it seemed to act as an aphrodisiac for us. It was no deterrent to our subsequent friendly liaisons with some young women of the island. The funny side of this is that I still associate garlic with the first exotic liaisons of my young life. It would seem that it would be a contradiction, but not in Africa.

The occasion of my eighteenth birthday took place on the second day that I was in Zanzibar. So, Hans and Gene decided that they would treat me to a grilled shish-kabob dinner, a manicure, a pedicure, and an active belly dance pro (offered to me with my meal as a special birthday treat). The night of my eighteenth birthday was a night for firsts for me. If I had not been so drunk on life, the heady ouzo I was not used to, and everything else, I would write more about it now. I tried my first marijuana cigarette (yes and I did inhale) and I enjoyed the beach and the company of beautiful girls. Haunting, was the combination of that first gyrating belly dance, pedicure, manicure, and the aroma of clove that permeated the warm, yet delightfully clean breezes coming softly ashore from the Indian Ocean. Ouzo, a licorice flavored liquor does not go well with Mary Jane, unless you're interested in becoming "blitzed." Up to that time, I never had been "blitzed." As I wrote previously, I grew up in a sheltered home where my dad drank nothing stronger than root beer and did not smoke anything at all. There was a red sunset that evening; it splashed streaks of purple, gold and blood red in my eyes and across pillowed soft clouds. Another unforgettable lifetime, "keeper memory" had been made. I occasionally see that scene in my dreams and when I think about my visit to Africa, as well.

We traveled all over the island of Zanzibar and I soon realized that I would have to procure a weapon for our defense and our ultimate survival. We had stopped at a copra plantation, where coconuts were being husked and the shells split to allow them to dry in the sun and then heated so oil could be extracted. The men worked with sharp, curved machetes. They did not like getting their pictures taken, nor did we surmise, that they did not like the way we looked, either. I felt this, for they looked at us with menacing eyes and made gestures with their machetes. These gestures indicated that if we did not beat a hasty retreat, they would do more than just warn us, they would attack. To this day, I could never figure out why they were so violently hostile to us. Perhaps it was because we were just foreigners, for we watched others take photos and they did not seem to notice or mind, but Gene and I somehow rubbed them the wrong way (maybe because we were both redheads. Note* many past Arab slavery taskmasters had red hair and beards)? According to the Index by anti-slavery Charity Walk Free Foundation (2013) who ranked 162 countries on the number of people living in slavery men, women and children; nearly 30-million people are living in slavery. It found that 10 countries accounted for 76-percent of the 29.8 million people living in slavery —India, China, Pakistan, Nigeria, Ethiopia, Russia, Thailand, the Democratic Republic of the Congo (very Democratic, eh?), Myanmar and Bangladesh. Modern slavery is defined as human trafficking, forced labor, and practices such as debt bondage, forced marriage and the incredibly egregious sale and exploitation of children. Flaunting your slaves in the Congo when we were there, was not "de rigueur", but we did see people who were slaves and were not allowed to talk to us-"when in Rome" what can you do, get into a knife fight?

On our third day, we visited the old slave quarters where the Arabs kept their booty of black slaves, bought and kidnapped from their tribes from East Africa and West Africa too. We saw the shackles and leg irons in the government building that had a huge medieval style door. We took photographs there and headed off to eat coconut husk-roasted snapper from the beach food vendors. They threw lines with a rock weight that disengaged, once the baits hit bottom. They pulled in beautiful Vermillion snappers, gutted them, put a spit though their mouths and out their vents and roasted them on the beach. WOW! Talk about fresh fish!

Zanzibar was a major slavery way station during the years that slavery was popular in the New and Old World, as it was down through history to the ancient Biblical, Egyptian and Roman times. Arab Taskmasters chained and mistreated so many of millions of blacks down through the centuries here, (as I stated above and am restating here) that perhaps seeing me and Gene's red beards and dress made them think we were Arabic. In any event, that experience came aboard my life as mental baggage for my entire life. Whenever I think of Zanzibar, that memory pops up. I am fortunate, the memory of the Hotel Pigale', Francine, its owner and the immeasurable beauty of that island, more than makes up for any negative memories of Zanzibar. The morning we left for Mombasa, we said adieu to Hans. He too was leaving that same morning for The Seychelles Islands. A couple of years later I received a postcard from Hans, it was a picture of me and Gene next to the big slavery door in the center of Zanzibar. He wrote in German that he went back to his iron business making decorative fencing. I never did see him again!

Gene and I visited the slave quarters belonging to the Muslims that sold over 750-thousand slaves brought from and through the mainland of Kenya and Tanganyika. . The door and shackles seen inside were all original to the building.

Zanzibar was originally settled by Africans about 3 or 4 thousand years ago. However, down through history; Assyrians, Sumerians, Persians, Indians, Egyptians, Chinese, Omari Arabs, Dutch, English and Portuguese put their dibs in on Zanzibar. The truth is traders, explorers, adventurers (I count myself as an adventurer) pirates and sultans found this island highly enchanting! I confess, because I was a young fellow and continually seeking out new and unusual places to visit, I was particularly taken by the mosque at Kizimikazi, which was built in the beginning of the 12th century and was, when I visited 52-years ago, as it is today; a big tourist attraction, not just due to its antiquity, but because it was such an interesting and ornately designed and built structure. Zanzibar was famous among Arabs as a trading place for ivory, slaves and spices. In 1832 Sultan Seyyid Said moved his Sultanate to Zanzibar, where his descendants ruled for another 130 years. Most of the wealth and land was in Arabic hands. I was there the last year of that sultan's family rule.

"Claudius Ptolomey wrote about Zanzibar in about 150 AD, about how it was a major Roman trade route to the Indo-Chinese harbors. The Indians, from India who settled on these Islands, were mostly shopkeepers and traders. The Portuguese were the first European settlers who ruled over Zanzibar. They held sway over Zanzibar for two hundred years.

In this period Dominicans, Jesuits and Augustinians wanted to convert the population of Zanzibar to Roman Catholicism and started to build churches. This attempt failed, because of the strong Muslim influence in Zanzibar.

97% of Zanzibar's population is Muslim; the other 3% are Catholics, Buddhist and Hindu. Although the Portuguese attempt to Christianize failed, there are still some relics of this time. These relics are bullfights on Pemba Island and some Swahili words. The Omani Arabs greatly influenced Zanzibar's culture and religion, which as I stated, is now mostly Islamic.

When Sultan Seyyid died, the British took over control of almost the whole island.

The British mostly came as missionary workers and attempted to abolish the slave trade in Zanzibar. Their attempts were mostly unsuccessful until 1890, when Sultan Ali freed all slaves. In this year Zanzibar and Pemba (a little island next to Zanzibar) were declared to be a British protectorate. This British protectorate lasted until Zanzibar's independence in 1963 just after we headed to the Kenyan mainland. Zanzibar gained its constitutional independence on 10 December 1963. In 1964 a bloody revolution began under the influence of John Okello. Okello and his supporters, mostly the black population of Zanzibar, were disappointed that the power was still in the hands of the Arab minority. Okello seized strategic government and police buildings and a radio station, from where he broadcast his revolutionary messages. In the course of the revolution approximately 17,000 of the Arabic and Indian population was killed.

That revolution ended with the declaration of a president from the Afro-Shirazi party. With the revolution, 200 years of Arabic authority over Zanzibar abruptly ended. Just a few months before we left Africa and on 24 April 1964 Zanzibar formed together with Tanganyika, now Tanzania, the United Republic of Tanganyika and Zanzibar. Today, Zanzibar is a semi-autonomous region of

Tanzania with its own President, First Minister, Cabinet and House of Representatives. " Wikipedia information-October-2013

A lot of things changed since the revolution. It seemed the early 60's; the time we were in Africa, was when many of the nations we visited were in flux, as far as their governments were concerned. Today, Zanzibar has an open and free market with a large advantage in the tourism business. Zanzibar is slowly building its own tourism and economic market.

Men and copra- These copra workers made threats to us after taking this photo. We guessed they did not like our red hair, perhaps thinking we were Arabs. Black Africans that we talked to thought of Arabs as "slavers."

From Zanzibar, we took a government launch the "approximate", 100 miles to Mombasa, Kenya. The cost for this trip was about $2.00 U.S.Mombasa is the seaside port city of Kenya, Africa. The trip back to the mainland from Zanzibar was rather uneventful, except for the spinner dolphins that were always fascinating and with the exception of when we arrived in Mombasa. At the port of Mombasa, we were met by a British Customs agent who also was the authority on who did, and who did not come into the country of Kenya. He was very officious, and when he asked me if I was indigent, I replied that my companion Gene was carrying all our funds, but we are sharing the money for the trip.

Coming in to Mombasa, Kenya by launch from Zanzibar in 1963.

He did not accept this, and insisted I had to be carrying my own funds. I had to prove to him that I would have the ability to live and leave the country under my own power and without becoming a burden to the country's coffers in any way. After much hassle and Gene having to change monies that were in his name on our American Express Travelers Checks into Kenyan Pounds, I put sufficient amounts into my pocket (about a hundred dollars). This would assure that the Brit would feel I would have enough cash to eat, rent a room and book passage out of the country. The British border guard finally allowed me to pass into the country. Very soon the British would be gone. A new era of Kenyan independence was closing in on the near-term, horizon.

The sights in Mombasa were most exciting. Commerce was being carried out on a large scale, but all was being done by hand. Humans were the main beast of burden. The variety of foodstuffs, textiles, trade wares, and livestock that were either being off loaded, or on- loaded to the many dhows and launches that were moored in Mombasa's Port, was staggering in their variety and tonnage.

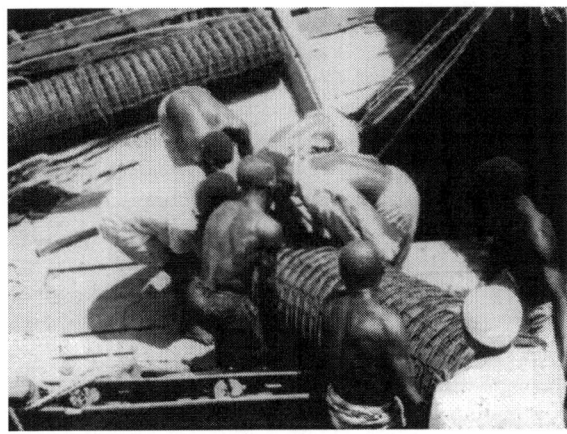

Black men sweating while loading goods −Commerce in Africa was always on the backs of local workmen. In this picture thousands of pounds of metal wire are unloaded or loaded each hour by the sweat of their brows.

We decided to preserve our capital, so we opted to stay in the local Young Men's Christian Association (YMCA) hostelry. This accommodation cost a mere one dollar per night for a clean cot and some semblance of bathroom facilities.

On the afternoon of our arrival and after settling in, we headed for the beach. As we walked on the beaches with soft clean, pure-white sands, a young man brought us a tiger conch shell after he made a short dive just off the shore. He cut its fastening operculum (foot), cleaned the shell out a bit and handed it to me for the sum of 10-cents. It was a large, beautiful shell and I wonder today if you can still find them near the beaches in Mombasa, I bet you cannot. We explored Mombasa and enjoyed our stay there. We found peoples from many nations doing a great deal of commerce in Mombasa, a port city, that for millenniums has seen the people, products, slaves from all points of the compass come and go from her shores. We had a dinner of fish heads in curry sauce for 20-cents, with a chunk of brown bread.

From Mombasa, we took a bus to Nairobi, the capital of Kenya, it cost about 25-cents per person. A gallon of gas was 20-cents and diesel was 15-cents (from my diary). We passed some wild looking veldt country. This was my first glimpse of a few of the wild African plains animals such as impala and wildebeests (many of which are mentioned in part two) of which I was to see a great abundance of on our trip further into my sojourn in east and central Africa, eventually in our own vehicle and in our own time. As a world traveler, I learned that if you can get by nicely with the local language, you're so far better off than a tourist that keeps asking everyone "do you speak English?" With this in mind, when I was in Israel, I found a book that translated English to Swahili and back. During my time in Israel it was far more enjoyable as I began to learn Hebrew and finally became 5th grade-proficient in the language; able to keep my hand-written diary in Hebrew script. The key to learning a foreign tongue is to speak it often, by associating with those that speak the language, not by associating with buddies that speak your language. So frequently traveling with a local, I made a point to tell him to speak "rock Evrit" (only Hebrew) and I would speak to him in German/Yiddish, as the Arab local wanted to go to German technical school and I wanted to become proficient in Hebrew. It worked! Together with daily classes, and speaking to locals, not hanging around with the Brits who only wanted to talk English, within 3-months I was talking Hebrew and understanding 95-percent of what I listened to. I believe that when you're in your youth, your brain can learn things and languages more easily than when you're in your 40's and older, if you apply yourself to the task. The first short sentence I learned in Swahili besides Jumbo (hello) was "mimi natacka maya" give me a glass of water! The Hebrew word for water is "mayim in Hebrew and maya in Swahili!" Do you see the connection?

The following is an updated look at the city of Mombasa and a bit of history for a place in Africa that has a history of more worldwide connectivity than perhaps anywhere else on the "Dark Continent": The city had a population of 939-thousand per the 2009 census, two times the population of when I was there decades ago and is located on Mombasa Island and the surrounding mainland's. The island is separated from the mainland by two creeks: The port serves both

44

Kenya and countries of the interior, linking them to the ocean. The city is served by Moi International Airport. Kenyan school history books place the founding of Mombasa as 900 A.D.

"Before the modern period, Mombasa was an important centre for the trade in spices, gold and ivory. Its trade links reached as far as India and China and oral historians today can still recall this period of local history. India history shows that there was trade links between Mombasa and Cholas of South India. Throughout the early modern period, Mombasa was a key node in the complex and far reaching Indian Ocean trading networks, its key exports then were ivory, millet, sesame products and coconuts. Today, with ivory off limits of harvest" Wikipedia information-October-2013

As I am closing the book on my book, this week; 2-tons of illegal ivory from poachers were uncovered at a dock in Mombasa. It was hidden in closed box containers in bags of sesame seeds and almost made it to boats taking this out of Africa for sale, or already pre-sold. Well, nearly 800-thousand slaves are traded each year to this very day. So is it any wonder there are those (just think of Somalia) that would continue to rob and kill off Africa's most natural resources for money? Pangolin scales for the species only found in sub-Saharan Africa and Asia were also discovered in the container. Pangolins have a body armor of scales and they are an animal that eats ants and termites. The scales are made into jewelry pendants and as an inlay on fine woodworking crafts. The containers had arrived into the country from Uganda by rail. Tudor went on to say: "We have stepped up the war on poachers to completely wipe ivory trade and poaching menace in the country that is threatening elephant population in the country and entire region." He said those behind the trade continue to advance the tactics of smuggling the ivory to avoid detection at the port. My opinion after getting to know a bit about how things in Africa really work is; it will never eradicate poaching in Africa! ." We came to Zanzibar from Tanganyika and then on to Mombasa on the same transport used throughout the ages, wind powered dhows.

AND THE KILLING AND MAIMING GOES ON AND ON

"Vasco da Gama was the first known European to visit Mombasa, receiving a chilly reception in 1498. Two years later, the town was sacked by the Portuguese. In 1502, the sultanate became independent from Kilwa Kisiwani and was renamed as Mvita (in Swahili) or Manbasa (Arabic). Portugal attacked the city again in 1528. In 1585 Turks led by Emir 'Ali Bey caused revolts from Mogadishu to Mombasa against the Portuguese landlords; only Malindi remained loyal to Portugal. Zimba cannibals overcame the towns of Sena and Tete on the Zambezi, and in 1587 they took Kilwa, killing 3,000 people. At Mombasa the Zimba slaughtered the Muslim inhabitants and had a buffet of them; but they were halted at Malindi by the Bantu-speaking Segeju and went home. This motivated the Portuguese to once again take over Mombasa a third time in 1589, and four years later they built Fort Jesus to administer the region. Between Lake Malawi and the Zambezi mouth, Kalonga Mzura made an alliance with the Portuguese in 1608 and fielded 4,000 warriors to help defeat their rival Zimba, who were led by chief Lundi. The Zimba with their tails between their legs retreated into obscurity, never again to attack the Mombasa area." Wikipedia information-October-2013

When we arrived in Nairobi after a dusty, bone-jarring bus ride, we promptly searched out a restaurant before anything else. We were starving following our bus journey, where it seemed that all day, nearly all the stops that we made, had a scarcity of foods that seemed fit enough for human consumption, often even without flies, most of it was not very appetizing.

In Nairobi, we found a courtyard restaurant with tropical trees that we had never seen before. There were flowers and shrubs that were totally different then we had encountered anywhere else. Everything I felt was quite foreign to me. Gene and I once again ordered some spicy Indian curry dishes of chicken and fish. After this meal we needed to imbibe at least a quart of liquids apiece. We had to water down the spices so we didn't burn out the lining of our esophagus, nor our stomachs, or later on the rest of our entrails. The food was good, and the curry necessary to keep it from spoiling, although spicy, was delicious too. Many of the extremely spicy foods you find in foreign nations are directly attributable, for the most part, to the lack of

46

available refrigeration. Thus, cuisine has evolved that takes into account heavy uses of spices (that's how French food was originally; spices and sauces to hide the smell, the appearance and kill the bacteria). These spices, besides adding flavor, really are preservatives and help keep the various ingredients from spoilage. Today, I still don't eat French cuisine; I want to get up close and personal with my meal with nothing hiding the main dish except a sprig of fresh picked herbs. The best thing I remember from that first Nairobi meal was the full-strength, large glass of passion fruit juice that cost a dime. I still remember how tasty and exotic the flavor was, no modern day dilution. The real thing!

Practically nothing can live in the spices of the orient, India, South America, and the African continent, because of the acids and alkaline produced by the various mixtures blended for food preservation. Our modern day foods that are processed, canned, and packaged contain a very high level of salt. This is the most ancient preservative that wars, battles and fortunes have been fought over down through the centuries. When we visited outdoor markets there was always a bulk salt seller available and also a fat seller. The fat was used to be rendered for cooking and it was sold as chunks and slabs to the homemaker-the cook. Africans had a terrible time finding and providing necessary food stuffs to keep themselves and their children healthy. We saw numerous goiter issues and distended children's stomachs everywhere we went.

After our meal, we sought out a hotel that was reasonably priced and yet in the heart of the Kenyan capital, Nairobi. We found a half-way decent hotel and set ourselves up to visit some of Gene's friends he had become acquainted with in Edinburgh, Scotland, when he was an exchange student there.

One gal, I remember very well, lived with her parents in Nairobi. Her father taught college level English to Kenyan teachers, and made his permanent home there. We visited the Evans for a home cooked meal for a change. We enjoyed the company of Carol, who had been a classmate of Gene's in Scotland-she was absolutely gorgeous! I ate steamed artichokes with lemon butter for the first time and met up with Simba, the Evans pet, full grown male lion with huge mane and teeth.

Just picture this: I was relaxing and eating a fabulous meal and suddenly turned around and found myself face to face with a lion that weighed upwards of 400 or more pounds, with three inch fangs just inches from my face. It looked at me and then tried to drown me by licking me with a 16-inch tongue. I actually first noticed that something was behind me was the odor of its breath, smelled sort of like a giant bellows spewing out old tuna fish cans left in the sun to marinate. Well, everyone laughed heartily when I, quite frightened down to my shorts, offered my entire plate of food to the lion to distract it from perhaps taking a bite out of me. Of course by that time I mostly realized that the lion was their pet and was just acting like a huge pussy cat. Nevertheless, I was certainly more than a bit taken aback, charmed and thrilled at the same time to be so close, in a seated, compromising position, which made me feel I had nowhere to run from the King of beasts. You could say I was running on pure amazement and outright terror.

Carols father assured me that Simba (Swahili for Lion) was always fed like she was a horse. Her appetite was satiated, or never let into the house, or near strangers-little comfort there! Things were different back then and there. I guess there were no laws governing zoning or just about any other law, other than the law of the land such as, not defecating in the street if anyone was watching, killing someone who didn't deserve it, throwing garbage out the window if someone was standing under the window, or having lions in your living room!

After dinner, I calmed down enough to play with the great cat and found that any rough housing I wished to initiate would most certainly be won by Simba. I was warned not to get too close with the cat that had 3-inch fangs and 4-inch, very sharp claws! Note* during my trip through Uganda, I was given a 3-inch fang tooth, that today has a pure gold cap with a ring for wearing it around my neck. A jeweler did this for me in 1964 in New York. It was quite affordable in 1964 at 130-per ounce.

At the same time we were in Kenya, the nation was about to become independent. Formerly, Kenya was a colony of Great Britain. England had agreed to allow Kenya to become independent and the English government and tribal chiefs sought a leader that could unite and represent all of the country.

Jomo Kenyatta was elected, and, because he was from the Kikuyu tribes, was feared because of the legacy of the dreaded Mau Mau issue. The Mau Mau, which was a Kikuyu founded terrorist group, advocated death and destruction to the colonials that had a strictly enforced stranglehold on the nation, as other colonials had done in the past. Robert Roark's book: "Uhuru," a Swahili word for "freedom," portrayed the Mau Mau movement in great detail--the Belgians in the Congo, the Italians in Ethiopia, the Boars of South Africa to name a few--colonists that effectively made slaves of the people. Arabs carried off the sold and stolen peoples of Africa to supply free labor to European, Arabic, and Western nations. This was done directly, and insidiously, as well. The destruction of tribal relationships (by dividing beliefs in tribal cultures) by missionaries appeared to me to be a great travesty that inspired great fear and hatred of foreign religious peoples, and white men in general. In the 1800's, Dr. Livingston worked in Tanganyika, he taught religion, but also was a doctor of the body, not just the soul. He, in those times was accepted and actually revered. It was a bit later on, when Stanley urged on after Stanley found Livingston, took over after the doctors passing (although if he was alive today, he would be hanged for what he helped King Leopold of Belgium do to the peoples of the Congo (see Congo chapter further on in the book). Today Stanleyville, Stanley Falls and Stanley Pool on the Congo River are named after the former newspaperman turned missionary, turned colonial agent for a King of Belgium.

The original close contacts with tribal Africa were those made by explorer missionaries. Missionaries were the chief reason for the division of son from the traditional ways of the father. Africans were directly made subservient to colonials. The infrastructure set up by the colonials, the missionaries, and merchants changed everything for the indigenous Africans. The monetary system, the social apartheid system, religion, an entire way of life, similar to what has happened to the American Indian was altered inextricably, for all time.

It was no wonder the Europeans were frankly, very frightened of what Kenyatta might do when he became president, and many were leaving (more like evacuating) very quickly.

The Italians seemed to have the biggest guilty conscience of all the Europeans we met. Italians were hated a great deal by all the Africans that I spoke to in my travels. These Italians (as were the Pakistani's) had a sordid history of rape and pillage in Ethiopia and Italians we traded with were quite frightened of the prospects of physical harm and expropriation of their properties and possessions. They left in droves, selling many of their possessions at a pittance of their worth.

It was at that time in Nairobi, Gene and I found our twenty dollar Land Rover that we used in our travels through the African continent. We walked the streets the day before the new President was sworn in during the morning. After our visit to the Evans's we found AGIP employees who worked for Italy's major petroleum corporation trying to get on any available airplane or ship back to Italy. While there, we met a long-time employee who was heading down, booking his ticket for that day's embarkation. He asked us if we would like to buy his Land Rover for fifty dollars. I haggled with him and got it for twenty dollars. That should show anyone reading this, how desperate those Italians with bad consciouses were to get out of town. I realized he would have just left it in the street if we had not come along, so desirous of getting out while the getting was good, so he made 20 dollars on the deal, after all.

The Land Rover had a winch worth four times more than what we paid for the vehicle and enough equipment that would allow us later to fiord streams, go just about anywhere we wanted to, as well as being able to cross muddy wadis with ease. By having a vehicle for the rest of our trip, basically for free, the price we could afford, we would be able to carry a whole range and array of trade goods that would allow us to barter for true native handcrafted goods that we wished to acquire as mementos of our trip and gifts for our friends and family. We did just that, and were able to bring home hand-made items that we all still treasure today over fifty years later. As we walked that street where we ultimately got that rover, there were MG's and Triumphs to be had for virtually nothing. However, I knew that we had to have a 4-wheel drive and not a sports car for our journey, no mufflers that are two inches from the ground and no storage space to boot! Oh, if I could only have those garages and have been able to have kept those sports car babies, now!

Our Land Rover & Gene checking out our trade booty. Without this vehicle I would be extremely doubtful if we'd have survived this journey.

After acquiring our rover and partially outfitting it for our ultimate trip into the interior, we left for Uganda. We wanted to leave too, before Kenyatta became president and we would become stuck in the gigantic festivities that would be Kenyans putting on for him and for themselves. After all, Kenyans were finally becoming independent. It was a long drive and a bit nerve wracking, leaving Kenya. Many locals we passed on our way to Kampala, the capitol of Uganda shook angry fists at us as we passed them along the highway. My garb consisted of a

British bush jacket, and we were driving a British Land Rover. When we were in Kampala, we painted letters on both sides of our vehicle in very large letters: " Etudians' De Estas Une" Students of the United States. We wanted to show that we were not military or any type of government people.

Later we heard that people did die during the celebrations. People shot their weapons off in the streets, a few took revenge on some of those they felt helped oppress them, or who worked too closely with the "Brits." Today, Kenyans have to worry about radical Muslims too! These Islamists have blown up hotels, murdered 67 people at a mall in Nairobi, murder and mayhem is their religion in Kenya, as it is worldwide. A Caliphate is sought by those intolerant of all others.

SOME HISTORY OF KENYA: OFFICIALLY THE REPUBLIC OF KENYA TODAY

We stopped each time we passed the equator, in east and central Africa, this stop was in the country of Kenya

"The capital and largest city in Kenya is Nairobi. Kenya lies on the equator with the Indian Ocean to the south-east, Tanzania to the south, Uganda to the

west, South Sudan to the north-west, Ethiopia to the north and Somalia (today a hot bed of Muslim terrorists) to the north-east. Kenya covers 224,445 square miles and has a population of about 44 million people in July 2012." Wikipedia information-October-2013

When we were in Kenya more than 50-years ago, the population was about 26-million. The population has doubled in 50-years. The country is named after Mount Kenya, the second highest mountain in Africa. When we left Mombasa, their major port city, we cut across the country, straight to Nairobi and did not take any side trips to the Masai Mara and to visit these interesting indigenous peoples of that famous area, the Masai. We wished we could have done so.

"Mount Kenya was originally referred to as "Mt. Kirinyaga" by the true natives of this area. "Kirinyaga or Kerenyaga, meaning 'mountain of whiteness' because of its snow capped peak"; the name was subsequently changed to Mt. Kenya because of the inability of the British to pronounce "Kirinyaga" correctly." The British never did get it! Wikipedia information-October-2013

The country has a warm and humid climate along its Indian Ocean coastline, with wildlife-rich savannah grasslands inland towards the capital. We traversed through this savannah on our way to Nairobi. Nairobi felt quite cool compared to where we had come from closer to the Indian Ocean. The cool climate gets colder approaching Mount Kenya, which has three permanently snow-capped peaks. Further inland there is a warm and humid climate around Lake Victoria, and temperate forested and hilly areas in the western region. The northeastern regions along the border with Somalia and Ethiopia are arid and semi-arid areas with near-desert landscapes. Lake Victoria, the world's second largest fresh-water lake and the world's largest tropical lake, is situated to the southwest and is shared with Uganda and Tanzania. I did want to fish there for giant Nile perch and huge Tiger fish, but just was not able to fit it in during our travels. I had to wait for our trip to the Congo for those Tiger fish.

Today, *Kenya is famous for its safaris and diverse wildlife reserves and national parks such as the East and West Tsavo National Park, the Masai Mara, Lake Nakuru National Park, and Aberdares National Park. There are several world heritage sites such as Lamu, and world renowned beaches such as Kilifi where today, international yachting competitions are held each year.* Wikipedia information-October-2013

We were in the country, when The Republic of Kenya became independent in December 1963 and in Nairobi when Kenyata was voted in as President. Following a referendum in August 2010 and adoption of a new constitution, Kenya is now divided into 47 semi-autonomous counties, governed by elected governors.

Nairobi is a regional commercial hub. Not being land locked from the ocean, has certainly helped the economy of Kenya that has the largest by GDP in East and Central Africa. Agriculture is a major employer and the country traditionally exports tea and coffee (lots of great coffee), and more recently fresh flowers to Europe. The service industry is a major economic driver.

During excavations at Lake Turkana in 1984, paleoanthropologist Richard Leakey assisted by Kamoya Kimeu discovered the Turkana boy, a 1.6 million year old fossil belonging to Homo erectus. Previous research on early hominids is particularly identified with Mary Leakey and Louis Leakey, who were responsible for the preliminary archaeological research at Olorgesailie and Hyrax Hill (we saw many Hyrax, in Kenya, and many years later in South Africa, they were all over the place, they look like large prairie dogs). Later work at the former site was undertaken by Glynn Isaac

Kenya has been inhabited by people for as long as human history has existed.

During the early Holocene period, the regional climate shifted from dry to wetter climatic conditions, providing an opportunity for the development of cultural traditions, such as agriculture and herding, in what became a more favorable environment for a variety of life. Without water, there are few opportunities for humans to think of anything else.

Arab traders began frequenting the Kenya coast around the 1st century AD.

The Kenyan coast had served host to communities of ironworkers and communities of subsistence farmers, hunters and fishers who supported the economy with agriculture, fishing, metal production and trade with foreign countries.

"In the centuries preceding colonization, the Swahili coast of Kenya was part of the east African region which traded with the Arab world and India especially for ivory and slaves (the Ameru tribe is said to have originated from slaves escaping from Arab lands sometime around the year 1700). Initially these traders came mainly from Arab states, but later many came from Zanzibar (such as Tippu Tip). Close to 90% of the population on the Kenya coast was enslaved. Swahili, a Bantu language with Arabic, Persian, Hebrew and other Middle Eastern and South Asian loanwords, later developed as a lingua franca for trade between the different peoples. Even today, there is an Arabic Slave trade and women for sex markets are a main target. Wikipedia information-October-2013"

COLONIAL ERA

"The colonial history of Kenya dates from the establishment of a German protectorate over the Sultan of Zanzibar's coastal possessions in 1885, followed by the arrival of the Imperial British East Africa Company in 1888. Germany handed its coastal holdings to Britain in 1890. This was followed by the building of the Kenya–Uganda railway passing through the country. This was resisted by some tribes — notably the Nandi Tribe, for ten years from 1890 to 1900 — however, the British eventually built the railway. The Nandi were the first tribe to be put in a native reserve to stop them from disrupting the building of the railway. During the railway construction era, there was a significant inflow of Indian peoples, who provided most of the skilled manpower needed for construction.

While building the railroad through Tsavo, a number of the Indian railway workers and local African laborers' were attacked by two lions known as the Tsavo man-eaters'. They and most of their descendants later remained in Kenya and formed the core of several distinct Indian communities such as the Ismaili Muslim and Sikh communities. A very exciting movie was made about these Tsavo man-eaters's.

During the early part of the 20th century, the interior central highlands were settled by British and other European farmers, who became wealthy farming coffee and tea. A major depiction of this period of change from one colonist's perspective is found in the memoir "Out of Africa" by Danish author Baroness Karen von Blixen-Finecke, published in 1937.) By the 1930s, approximately 30,000 white settlers lived in the area and gained a political voice because of their contribution to the market economy. The area was already home to over a million members of the Kikuyu people, most of who had no land claims in European terms, and lived as itinerant farmers. To protect their interests, the settlers banned the growing of coffee, introduced a hut tax, and the landless were granted less and less land in exchange for their labor. A massive exodus to the cities ensued, as their ability to provide a living from the land dwindled. By the 1950s, the white population numbered 80,000.

In 1952, Queen Elizabeth II and her husband Prince Phillip were on holiday at the Treetops Hotel in Kenya when her father, King George VI, passed away in his sleep. The young princess cut-short her trip and returned home immediately to take her throne. Queen Elizabeth II was crowned at the Westminster Abbey in 1953 and, as one gentleman put it, she went up a tree in Africa a princess, and came down a queen. From October 1952 to December 1959, Kenya was under a state of emergency arising from the Mau Mau rebellion against British rule. The governor requested and obtained British and African troops, including the King's African Rifles. The British began counter-insurgency operations; 10-years before we were in Kenya, in May 1953 General Sir George Erskine took charge as commander-in-chief of the colony's armed forces, with the personal backing of Winston Churchill

The capture of Warũhiũ Itote (aka General China) on 15 January 1954 and the subsequent interrogation led to a better understanding of the Mau Mau command structure. Operation Anvil opened on 24 April 1954, after weeks of planning by the army with the approval of the War Council. The operation effectively placed Nairobi under military siege, and the occupants were screened and the Mau Mau supporters moved to detention camps. The Home Guard formed the core of the government's strategy as it was composed of loyalist Africans, not foreign forces like the British Army and King's African Rifles. By the end of the emergency, the Home Guard had killed 4,686 Mau Mau, amounting to 42% of the total insurgents. The capture of Dedan Kimathi on 21 October 1956 in Nyeri signified the ultimate defeat of the Mau Mau and essentially ended the military offensive. During this period, substantial governmental changes to land tenure occurred. The most important of these was the Swynnerton Plan, which was used to both reward loyalists and punish Mau Mau. Wikipedia information-October-2013

I highly recommend the book; "Uhuru by Robert Rourke. It depicts how the Mau Mau used terror tactics to scare the farmers off their lands which the farmers mainly had taken from the Mau Mau in the first place.

Kampala University view from roof looking towards Lake Victoria. I climbed to the roof of American University in Kampala Uganda to take this image of part of the campus with Lake Victoria in the background.

Traveling past the Kenyan, Ugandan border without incident, we stopped on the White Nile River Bridge that was also a hydroelectric dam. We took pictures of the hippos in the still waters of the upper part of the dammed river across the road from the dam. We also looked over the dam into the giant turbulent pool below. I saw a fisherman with bulging muscles fighting a very large fish, using a long, sturdy bamboo pole of at least fourteen feet in length. He dragged a giant fish out onto the rocky shore and I just had to get down there to see what it was and try my hand at this fishing.

The fisherman was catching giant carp and catfish. These big fish weighed forty to fifty pounds and up, each. I enjoyed watching him walk into the water, drop his cornmeal ball bait, and when a big fish took it, lift his large pole in an arch. With straining muscles, he'd drag the fish straight out of the water as quickly as possible. It was quite a sight, and my little Japanese reel and solid fiberglass rod were not up to the job and could not hold any of these fish in the turbulent swift currents. My line broke every time.

Continuing on to Kampala, the capitol of Uganda, we found a small penchant to bed down in. It was here we provisioned more fully for our trip into the interior. Here we dealt with Indian merchants and they were reasonably fair and great bargainers, although as stated before, we found out the Ugandan natives hated them due to jealousy of their economic success and also because the Indians held themselves aloof, for the most part from the African population.

CHAPTER FOUR

THE KARAMOJA UGANDA TRIP TO THE SUDAN

On the ship from Israel, we met a young man whose family lived in Kampala Uganda (the capitol city of Uganda). His father worked in the Israeli Embassy and his son told us that he would act as our guide when we eventually reached Uganda. He would take us to the Northern areas of the country, the part of Uganda that bordered the country of Sudan. When we eventually got to Uganda, we looked him up and true to his word; he guided us on a trip to this very wild, desert area, where he previously had a chance to visit.

This area was known as the "Karamoja", Land of the Karamojong peoples Nomadic Warriors. When we arrived into the area, it looked and gave you the feeling that you had gone back into the prehistoric era. The blazing heat of the desert plains offered up heat waves and illusions on our ride into the past. We were actually viewing a landscape full of numerous mirages. Any moment, I felt that a huge land sloth or giant lizard would come lumbering, or slithering out of the shimmering light from behind an acacia tree, and the sparse shade, that it offered. And then I saw that giant lizard-not!

In Karamoja, we stopped to photograph local nomadic peoples wherever we found them.

As we drove towards the country border with Sudan, we saw vultures circling in the distance and decided to investigate by going off the road in our four-wheel-drive, 1955 Land Rover. We came upon a dead zebra, wild dogs hung back and several hyenas fed on the carcass. We startled them as we drove up, but perhaps because they were used to being photographed and seeing vehicles before, they didn't scatter very far. We sat and watched as the vultures, settled down to dipping their heads into the belly cavity and rib cage of the carcass, fighting and jostling each other for a chance at the macabre meal. The wild dogs moved in every few minutes and snatched bits and pieces for themselves, until the hyenas finally built up enough courage to disregard our potential and perceived threat and chased both the vultures and dogs away so they could continue to feed. We knew that what we witnessed was elemental nature at its best or worst depending on your perspective. I for one, felt like a voyeur into the world as it was and as it had been before man walked the earth, or at the very least when he first walked on this planet as a true man. The experience was profoundly moving to a youth who had been brought up in a society that has been refined down to meats in plastic packages, homogenized or powdered milk in red cartons and cans, paved roads, greenery that had tamed, man-made borders containing their wildness in a domesticity that left little to the imagination.

Seeing the sights of wild Africa seemed to open a window to a past, that is part of a collective unconscious that, masked by the trappings of modern technology, had kept my hunter instincts just beneath the surface, then to have been temporarily unleashed by this experience. I relished it; I tingled in sort of a hair-stiffening, on-my-back, kind of feeling. Somehow, I felt a bit wilder and freer for just a few moments in time.

We headed for an area that was inhabited by many of the African plains animals such as: zebra, giraffe and antelopes. We later saw these animals in the Ruwenzori Game Park and other established, yet very wild parks in those years, that we needed to traverse throughout our travels. We never saw any people in these parks, no vehicles, just elephants, Cape buffalo and millions of antelopes of several varieties.

Further along in our trip, we discovered that the zebra we found earlier had probably been killed by those hyenas. We thought it was a lion kill, but a Brit who hunted the Karamoja told us that the hyenas were every bit as deadly as and perhaps even more so than the lions.

The Karamojan peoples that we met were very tall and appeared to be descended from the Watusi, (Tutsi's) or related to the Watusi of Rwanda and the Congo. When we met these nomadic men and women, clad only in loincloths and who had all their possessions hung on a belt around their waists or carried on top of their heads, we thought they were Tutsi's. After researching their history we now believe they migrated into the area from the Sudan. These possessions hanging from their belts, included curious little wooden stools with legs, and some rounded bases that these people used as pillows and as seats to keep their private parts and their ears, noses and throats respectively, from being crawled in and on by insects of the night and day. We traded for these artistically crafted little stools and collected several different variations of these beautiful hand-crafted art forms to us, yet practical and useful items to the Karamojan's. Small ornate stools similar to the ones we traded for can be seen in the Smithsonian Museum as part of ancient Egyptian exhibits. The Karamojan's also had handmade knives and some clothing and sundry domestic items which the men carried on a belt, and the women, as was custom throughout our travels, carried on their heads. Bare-breasted, tall and proud-looking Karamojan women struck an unusually beautiful pose against the stark desert background of the Karamojan desert. The brass adorning their necks was made with telegraphic wires that their men gave to them after taking down cross-country communications.

During our travels to this Northern area of Uganda, we came very close to the border with Sudan and arrived at a prison. The prison warden allowed travelers in to a special store area, where handmade items crafted by the inmates could be purchased. These hand crafted items were made by prisoners, who were incarcerated for every crime known to man; including political crimes against the immediate, yet temporary rulers of the government (Idi Amin took over next door in Uganda and had everyone killed that did not agree with him, a bit later on after we were long gone). These inmates, just like the license plate makers in American prisons, earn their keep by making tribal animal skin covered drums, spears, medicine masks, African musical instruments and woodcarvings. I preferred to trade in the jungles and hinterlands, but we did buy a couple of interesting skin covered drums, there.

During our travels through, over and along the dusty, rutted roads of this area, we stopped frequently to look at exotic trees and bushes such as the giant and curious cucumber tree, with large inedible cucumber like fruits hanging down to the ground, alongside the road. We saw several varieties of flowering cacti; they showed us a rainbow of colors that seemed to have been painted by Picasso.

Driving along, we would suddenly come across giraffes that towered above some of the acacia trees, which they fed on. Herds of zebra would suddenly race across the road in front of us, and I would brake and come to an abrupt stop and marvel at the sight of thundering hoofs kicking up dust all around us. Occasionally, impala would prance alongside the road, being chased by predators or perhaps just frightened by our vehicle.

These nomadic Karamojan women were gathering lizards and snakes to feed their families with. Note the copper metal rings around their necks. This wire is fashioned from telegraph wires that were pilfered off long distance telegraph poles.

We had passed safely over a bridge one day and returning the next day, we found that same bridge washed out. Auto's not equipped as we were with our four-wheel Land Rover, were stranded and backed up near the bridge, unable to fiord the swift water that was caused by sudden overnight heavy thunderstorms. After assessing the situation, I climbed up and along a walkway railing that did not wash away with the bridge, and affixed a cable from our winch to a sturdy tree trunk across the swollen brook. I went back, started the winch and dragged our Land Rover, across the stream with Gene behind the wheel, to the accompaniment of envious stares, by those that were not similarly equipped, and remained trapped on the other side.

Continuing on back towards the Uganda capitol of Kampala, we came across a family cooking a stew over a bright red-hot fire. We approached and saw that they had lizards and other animals they had captured and gathered for their subsistence meal, that was their fare probably since time began. We were invited to join in out of courtesy and hospitality, but Gene and I had a difficult time doing so because we were just not ready to take on foods that hadn't been cleaned and processed, or at least had their bowels and intestines removed. This was not the case later on in our trip when we ate things that today, I wouldn't even think of touching-acute hunger can make you do things otherwise.

Our Israeli friend bartered as we did, for handmade items that were beautifully crafted by the Karamojans from natural and man made items.

One thing we learned the hard way in Africa was, that refusing the hospitality of a shared repast, was an insult to those that invited you to "break bread" so to speak, with them. Another formality was belching and displaying other natural body noises such as flatulence, which was expected and was a clear sign to your hosts that all was well and acceptable and it proved satiation to all around you. So when we understood this, we belched out loud often, after each and every meal.

That is, the meals we had obtained and could get to stay down, the victuals we did not have to sneak under the table to the dogs in waiting. The most difficult items to eat during our trip through equatorial Africa were: monkey brains, some snakes, rotted fish, worms, pupae (live or roasted) and some lizards. Overall, the reptiles were great roasted, once properly cleaned, but the monkey was just too close to our lineage for us not to feel like we were not cannibals. Besides, we didn't like the gamey taste, or smell either.

Selling, actually bartering monkey along the road. I just took a picture, not the monkey! Meat was scarce in the Congo. No stores, you got it where and when you could. That stick was his store.

We came to a small village and stopped because we saw a cat in a cage near the side of the road. It turned out it was a young Cheetah and it was for sale. They told us its mother was killed by a lion. I fell in love, in spite of Gene warning me it would be a mistake for us to travel with a Cheetah, but I was smitten with this large kitten! I bought the spotted, gorgeous cat for the equivalent of 5-bucks! Seems, they didn't want to feed it, they wanted the lizards that they were feeding it, for their children's meals. They were poor and malnourished then, and 52-years later more than 45-percent of the children still are. I was afraid the cheetah would turn into a pair of slippers, or an arrow quiver. I was 18-years old and up for anything, except, that as we drove out of town with cheetah in tow in the back seat, it wanted out of the vehicle and scratched my back as if I was the upholstery trying to get a foot hold for jumping out the front window, which it did. It scampered into the bush and I never saw it again. I tried to look for it, but because of the fear of snakes or other critters I might encounter, I chalked it up to one of those experiences you never forget! I never forgot that incident; it taught me a valuable lesson: wild things, no matter how much one would like to tame them, really remain inherently wild. You cannot take the wild out of an animal that has been hard-wired through the ages to be just that; wild! One would have to break the spirit of an animal to domesticate; that which just cannot be truly domesticated and should not be, either. I am loathe to see wild animals in zoo's and being trained to please peoples curiosity; that goes for all wild animals everywhere. My plan for that cheetah kitten was to eventually return it to the wild once it had some maturity under its fur. I believe it never did grow up to reach speeds of 70-mph as an adult. I feel it was killed by other wild critters. But at least it did not turn into a wallet or pocketbook!

When we returned from our Karamojan adventure, we again rented a room in a penchant type of a motel-an early African hotel kind of place. We had two beds, and a bathroom that was open to the bedroom. It had high ceilings and was quite comfortable as well as eminently affordable.

From here we ventured out to shop for our Congo trip, picking up various trade goods such as cartons of Belgian cigarettes, razor blades, nail clippers and all kinds of pocket and fixed blade knives and pocket mirrors. We also stocked plenty of Coca-Cola, but later found the bottles were worth far more in trade than the nasty liquid inside them. So after we drank or cleaned our tires and bumpers (warm Cokes, ugh!) we saved the bottles and found them to be very valuable for trading in the Congo. It seems that the natives of the jungle love them and made carrying straps out of wicker and monkey hides. The bottles with a carved stopper made great poison arrow dispensers or medicine bottles, and the poison liquids in them did not dry out, as they did in locally grown and dried, gourd containers. We also stocked up on food stuffs. We bought a little finger- can opener and the cans we planned on opening were the small sized Campbell Beans-boxes of them, also we traded for two large stalks of red bananas that we ate as they ripened along the way. Boxes of Belgian salt crackers, jars of peanut butter were stocked too! For water we purchased Halazone tablets for purification. We kept a canvas water bag bottle slung over the front of the rovers hood. As we traveled, the water bag allowed for evaporative cooling of the water as it traveled in the wind of our vehicle movement. No matter what, the water tasted horrible, but when you're thirsty in a tropical heat, it begins to taste like the finest champagne.

I decided to buy this cheetah, but the cheetah had Uhuru (freedom) on its mind. After driving a distance with the cat, it jumped out the window of our vehicle, scampered into the woods, and was never seen again.

One evening, we went to a movie theatre with two dates- two local young women that took a fancy to us from the college. "The Longest Day" movie with John Wayne was playing and the theatre was packed. We had gone in with lots of food stuffs, popcorn and sweet candies, after smoking a bit of Mary Jane. Things went nicely, until that Nazi soldier in the movie came at a soldier with a bayonet on that large screen. In my drug fogged brain, I believed the soldier was attacking me and I jumped backwards out of my seat into the lap of an Indian woman with a big red dot on her temple. She was sitting all dressed up next to her husband and he completed the stupid scene we made, by pushing and punching at me. Saying I'm sorry, I clocked him hard on the jaw. We were ejected and never saw that movie again, until decades later on HBO. Our dates thought it all amusing, as we spoke in both English and broken Swahili to them, explaining that I had never had a marijuana cigarette before and certainly could not hold it, as I could not hold my liquor either. I was definitely a very cheap date. One rum punch and I danced on anyone's table. We all danced that night in Kampala!

Unfortunately, the next day Gene and I walked past the big Coca Cola billboard and a street vendor was selling half bags of marijuana for 50-cents each. We bought two bags! That evening, alone in our room, we emptied out a Marlboro cigarette of its tobacco and stuffed it with what we thought was marijuana. It was not! Turned out, it was opiated hashish. We smoked it and had horrible experiences, losing our minds that night. I broke up the room, begged G-D to restore my cloudy, and afflicted brain to normal from a raving maniac, between, flashing moments of lucidity. I tore out the plumbing from the sink, broke the mirror and made a dagger out of a long shard and tore up my pillow to eat the feathers mixed with blood, I caused to well-up on Gene's chest, by cutting a tic tac toe board into it. The effect of the drugs on Gene, was that he basically became catatonic, his eyes rolled back under his upper lids and as I recall, my memory jogged by my diary, he somewhat seemed to feel no pain, nor protested as I wiped the blood with feathers and began eating them. I floated above the room, looking down on myself and my actions. I begged G-D during those short, very short lucid moments to give me back my brain. I made so much noise, that the building manager called the police. They broke in, beat me silly and dragged both our butts to a smelly jail cell.

Of course a few bucks fixed anything over there, and when we came to our senses in the miserable morning, we paid off, to bail out of this little hell-hole. We were able to get our things, paid off the manager for repairs and sought out another temporary abode. We found another place to live. This time we stayed away from dope and dopers, until much later on in a different world, we found the Pygmies.

This man was selling all kinds of ground up animal parts for curatives and he sold us what we thought was marijuana. It turned out to be opium infused hashish and it was responsible for me and Gene going stark raving mad one night in our Kampala Uganda room.

After heading out for a bite of lunch, we met a student at the American University in Kampala. She invited us to visit the school, meet her teachers as well as some student friends and have lunch there. It was a beautiful edifice with striking views from the elevated walkways between buildings and that experience was our best in Kampala. We were there before Idi Amin came to power. The place was a true microcosm of a democratically operating, free-trade, capitalistic country. A few years later, Idi Amin came to power and turned Uganda into a nasty police state. The damages done and amount of people destroyed are still today not completely known. His soldiers also killed off much of the wildlife in Uganda to feed themselves. Amin didn't feed the soldiers. The low-life fed himself and his family lavishly at the expense of his people! The true story about Entebbe, with the most beautiful jungle gardens in the world (Johnny Weissmuller made his Tarzan movies here) was a "cause celeb" when the Israeli IDF fooled Amin and his cutthroats and rescued those hostages that the Arabs hijacked for shock effect, to hurt and extort the Israelis. Amin knew that Israel was a friend to Uganda in so many ways, not the least of which concerned the health of the peoples; Israel, having sent numerous doctors to Uganda during times of disease outbreaks over the years, and yet he took the terrorists side and made himself the laughing stock of the world. All the so-called Palestinians did for Amin's people were a big fat "nothing." Except make Amin appear the clown he was, to the rest of the world.

Besides bananas, small cans of beans, various wonderful tropical fruits such as guava, papaya, mango, and the aforementioned bananas (the little red variety, so sweet, so good) we also availed ourselves of the local fare: For main dishes when we were invited by locals for meet and greets, the meals usually centered on a sauce or stew of groundnuts, beans or meat. We tried to avoid meats whenever possible except for chicken and snake. Why not meat, we just didn't know where it came from, how fresh and healthy it was, did it have worms or flukes, bacterial issues, so we tried to avoid it! The starch we mostly enjoyed, traditionally came from ugali (maize meal) or matoke (boiled and mashed green banana) when we were in the South, or an ugali that was made from millet in the Northern part of Uganda. Cassava, yam and; a so-called African sweet potato (actually an American Indian root crop vegetable) are also eaten; when we were invited to a more affluent household, our meals often included white (often called "Irish") potato and rice. We did not experience eating Soybeans in our diet; these were promoted as a healthy food staple in the 1970s and are also used especially for breakfast. Chapatti, an Asian flatbread, reminded us greatly of Pita we had in Israel and staple bread all over the Mideast, was also part of Ugandan cuisine. I could have lived on that bread, with or without anything covering it!

We left Kampala several days later after recuperating from our drug induced misery and my lumps and bumps from a policeman's baton. We headed for the border crossing at northwestern tip of Uganda and the Belgian Congo. We first stopped into the Chinese Embassy to get a Trip-tique, Voyage Passé (basically a sort of visa) into the Congo. The young, diminutive and cute passport checker warned us in no uncertain terms, not to touch any diamonds we would be offered throughout our trek across the country. She said we should not go to the Congo, echoing what the British soldiers had told us in Tanganyika. She more or less begged us to listen to her, as she said in broken English: "you nice boys need to be careful, or you die in the Congo." We tried to listen to her! But we failed. We did go to the Congo, but we listened to the part about never buying or trading for diamonds.

A BIT ABOUT UGANDAN HISTORY

"Uganda, officially the Republic of Uganda, is a landlocked country in East Africa. Uganda is bordered on the east by Kenya, on the north by South Sudan, on the west by the Democratic Republic of the Congo, on the southwest by Rwanda, and on the south by Tanzania. The southern part of the country includes a substantial portion of Lake Victoria shared with Kenya and Tanzania. Uganda lies within the Nile basin, and has a varied but generally equatorial climate." While we were there, we experienced very comfortable temperatures and we were there before the rainy season.

"Uganda takes its name from the Buganda kingdom, which encompasses a large portion of the south of the country including the capital Kampala. The people of Uganda were hunter-gatherers until 1,700 to 2,300 years ago, when Bantu-speaking populations migrated to the southern parts of the country."

The author standing both on the north and south side of the Equator marker in Uganda.

Beginning in the late 1800s, the area was ruled as a colony by the British, who established administrative law across the territory. Uganda gained independence from Britain on 9 October 1962. The period since then has been marked by intermittent conflicts, most recently a lengthy civil war against the Lord's Resistance Army, which has caused tens of thousands of casualties and displaced more than a million people. Yet another debacle, one or more in every nation we visited in Africa.

The official language in Uganda is English, but we had to speak Swahili (I had to) Gene did not learn Swahili) to get directions and easily communicate with most everyone, outside of the capitol city.

We headed through a huge game park; the Ruwenzori, on our way to the border crossing and slept under our Land Rover once again, before plunging ahead to the border. I awoke at just before dawn to a strange hissing and gurgling, rumbling sound. It was a bull elephant sniffing our feet sticking out from under our vehicle. This giant looked even more gigantic when I swung around and looked up at this monster with huge ivory tusks, sticking out of the side of its mouth! That experience truly scared me, even though we realized that the behemoth was curious and sniffing us out. Thinking back, I guess to the elephant, we were two big garlic cloves sandwiched between the ground and a muffler. No damage, no hits, fouls or errors. The trip to the border was without incident except for the pachyderm visit. Oh, yes another few special encounters and experiences on the way to the border we planned on crossing through to get into the Congo: As we drove along through the game park, I stopped the vehicle when I saw a herd of Cape Buffalo browsing a couple of thousand feet off the roadway. I got out of the rover to protestations by Gene that getting too close to these mean tempered mini-locomotives on hooves would be too dangerous for me. Young blood does young, hot blooded things sometimes. So I didn't listen to anything but my Brownie camera that kept saying: "shoot me, shoot me, and get that photo", so I walked down a short hill from the vehicle and then a longer sloping hill. I misjudged just how far the buffalo were and I came up to the top of the hill and a little rise just over it, there I was face to face with these big smelly animals. They immediately saw me and I stopped dead in my tracks, not even holding up the camera as I did so. Slowly, very slowly I raised the camera to eye-level, spotted through the viewfinder, clicked the shutter release just once and then began backing up, very, very slowly. These were days when there were not as many safaris' going on in that game park, so I believed that the buffalo, although not aggressive, yet to me, were as curious about me as I was about them. They snorted, but never put their ears back and certainly didn't charge me. If they had, I would have been a goner. They can run at 30-miles per hour and me, heck maybe I could have made 3-mph on those hills. I heard Gene yelling from the vehicle for me to get back quickly, but I instinctively knew to go slow and steady and not run. I made it back unscathed to the vehicle and Gene was quite perturbed at me for taking that chance. I made light of it, especially due to the fact that I made it back as that legendary animal tamer and trainer, Frank Buck would say: "I brought em' (my butt cheeks) back alive!"

I wasn't being brave just foolish. If I had gotten any closer to these Cape Buffalos and they charged I would have been a goner! Shooting a Kodak Brownie with no zoom I had to get close to get any kind of decent image.

In that same game park, further on down the road towards the Congo border, I saw a bull elephant near a tall acacia tree reaching up to strip leaves for its meal. Again I stopped the vehicle and began an approach so as not to spook the elephant-out in the open and singing On Top of Old Smokey. Gene was beside himself with anger at my bold move. He told me that I was not only jeopardizing my life but his whole trip. If anything happened to me, it would be all over and shipping my body back to New York would break his budget. Imagine that, he was worried about the budget! Well, really, we had become very close pals already and I do believe he really was afraid for me and that was it! Of course I didn't listen, so I slowly made my way away from the Land Rover and towards the elephant with my little fixed lens, Kodak Brownie Camera and black and white AGFA film. The elephant had its back to me for awhile, but then it became aware of me by nose and sound. If you will recall, I smelled like a giant crushed, walking garlic clove and my boots always found something to crack under foot. I was not a Pygmy or a Masai hunter; I was a babe in the woods! So the elephant turned in my direction and was facing me, I tried to get closer, as I knew just shooting the camera wasn't going to get me a decent image of the elephant, more like a throw-away photo. So, I kept on trecking on! This time the elephant let me know without any doubt of its displeasure of my encroachment in his territorial imperative. The elephant trumpeted loudly, and Gene back at the rover later said he figured it was all over. Due to the fact that I was totally in the open and if the elephant charged with serious intent to do away with this bothersome, smelly human all he had to do was run me down and break my back with a swipe of its trunk, or a crushing step, or head press on my little body. It did neither, it just warned me, so I stopped moving in its direction, slowly raised the camera and clicked the shutter. You would have thought I shot at the elephant. That tiny clicking noise was magnified on that open veldt to almost sound like a shot from a rifle to that elephant. It bluff charged me; thank god it was just a bluff. After kicking up some dust, flaring its ears and humping up its back, yelling at me that piercing shrill, but incredibly loud trumpeting roar, with its trunk high in the air, it very thankfully backed off. But, the big, around 12-thousand pound pachyderm kept watching me intently. I believe now that if I had taken one more step in its direction it would have charged me in earnest. Frankly, I was thrilled but too foolish to really be scared! I should have been. But with Gene yelling at me back at our vehicle, and the fact that I thought I had gotten a decent photograph, I backed up too! Very slowly, I kept walking backwards singing "Love is a Many Splendid Thing" then I tripped over a shrubs root and fell backwards. I heard a yell from Gene, looked through my boots tips facing the air and saw the elephant running at me. If I wasn't so scared and in a fight or flight mode I would have checked my pants for an accident. Forget the fight, I turned and ran hell-bent towards the rover, Gene ran a bit to the side of the vehicle and jumped up and down waving his hands trying to distract the big beast. It seemed to work, he was on the road and higher up than the elephants head was and I believe today, he probably saved me because the elephant broke off its run at me, turned abruptly and began heading back away from us.

This Bull Elephant and I got a bit too close for comfort. I left the vehicle to get a good photo and was lucky the elephant did not see me as a serious threat. It did begin telling me with sound and body language that it did not like hearing the click of the camera.

TRAVELING THE DIRT ROAD ROUTES FROM UGANDA TOWARDS THE CONGO

Before we even got into the Congo, still in Uganda, there we were, at the mercy of border guards, with the education of a nursery school grade child back home in the states. They had the final decision to let us pass from one country to another, based on paper work they could not read, and the amount of bribe they would accept. For the most part, the Africans could get us through any checkpoint with no problems; however the Pakistani born guards, who were British trained, hated us immediately the minute they spotted our visa tickets from Israel on our passports. That was a horse of a different breed altogether! They not only made it hard for us, they wanted us to suffer. It was like the time we got to a Northern border checkpoint and tried to pass into the Congo. The following is an account of this episode that Gene and I experienced at this border crossing:

After traveling from Kampala, the capital city of Uganda through vast areas of plains and woodlands loaded with wildlife on our way to the Congolese border of Usuru, we stopped at a checkpoint to inquire about passing over to the Congolese side. There we met a Pakistani border guard and his black, local Ugandan assistant. We were told that we could cross the border, but we could not take our Land Rover unless we left a $500 deposit in American dollars, which would be refunded on our return to this border. We tried in vain to explain that we were traveling through Africa as medical students, and we could not be sure that we would come back through, and besides $500 American was all the funds we had for our trip. I remember clearly how the Pakistani border patrol person responded to us with a cold heartless leer "take the other road, 300 miles to the next border, maybe they will let you through for $50 American." Of course we were stunned, and because we did not have the ability to pay the money, we had a dilemma on our hands, that at the time seemed insurmountable. We devised a plan: Gene would walk across the border and speak to the Congolese guards on their side of the border. He would see how they felt about letting us come in their country by driving in at full speed. After bribing them with ten dollars, he walked back across the border to where I sat guarding the Land Rovers from vandalism and theft with my double-edged sword. The plan we concocted, was to bribe the Ugandan African guard on the Uganda side of the border. Then when the Pakistani went to bed at midnight, I would crash the barriers with our vehicle, and race across to the Congolese side without bullets whistling past my ears, or finding their mark in my body. We paid the guard 35 dollars in American currency. Gene was to walk across to the Congolese side later that evening, and I was to start the engine, race down the hill, and crash the barrier; speeding the quarter mile to the other border, where Gene would identify me and the vehicle to the guards. Then Gene would jump into the rover and we would be off. Well, everything seemed to be working perfectly, the guard gave me the "go ahead" sign based on his superior having gone to bed at midnight. Gene was over on the Congolese side, and all I had to do was start the rover and race through the barrier and we would be "home free".

I pressed the start button on the rover and it rumbled to life, the roar of its engine was suddenly deafening to me. It seemed that in the still of the night, except for peeper frogs, the noise would wake the dead, let alone the Pakistani. I looked up at the hill where the house was and saw the lights coming on. Shoving the rover gearshift forward, I popped the clutch, and raced for the barrier. Just then, out of the corner of my eye, I spotted the African rifle coming up, and he seemingly took aim at my head. All of a sudden, as I came close to the barrier, the rover engine sputtered then died, so without power I glided closer to the barrier. Without the forward momentum and power of the engine, I knew I couldn't make it to the other side of the barrier, so I stopped just short of it and frantically tried to re-start the engine but to no avail. I thought of "Murphy's Law" and began laughing, by then the Pakistani was by the side of the vehicle, and a handgun and the Africans rifle were inches from my ear. I then begged real hard not to be killed.

The River between Uganda and the Congolese border

In the meantime, Gene, from his vantage point across the border and river, had heard the engine start-up, cough and then die. He waited just a moment and then, when he was sure I had been detained, he walked back across the border to where I was being threatened with death by the Pakistani. We were arrested and locked in a mud building, and were told that the next day we had to leave the border area and drive back to Uganda. The African border guard watched what was happening to us and knew what was going to happen, so I asked him for the 35 dollars back or else I would tell the Pakistani of his collusion with us. He promptly complied with our request, for he knew that trouble with us crazy Americans "was-a-brewin". This African border guard, in all fairness, was very sympathetic with us before we tried our ill fated border crossing attempt, and I remember how he said, "We Ugandan's used to handle our own affairs, and the British were responsible for letting these foreigners (referring to the Indians and Pakistani's) come into our country, and take away the good jobs and practically make us economic slaves to their wishes." Footnote: when Idi Amin came into power he expelled all the Indians and Pakistani's and took their properties. Apparently what this guard had told us was true, for the Africans everywhere we traveled seemed to resent (actually hated) the Indians and Pakistani's with a vengeance. The Ugandan told us that the reason he tried to help us besides the American dollars, was due to the fact that his mother, a year back was saved by an Israeli doctor from dying, due to a disease she contracted (average life span of Ugandans today 53, in 1962, it was late 40's) and when he offered to help us, it was as if repaying a debt. He said when he tried to pay the doctor; the doctor smiled and said "no, seeing your mothers smile was payment in full." I guess what goes around comes around; I've never forgotten the face of that Ugandan when he talked to us about that incident. I really believe today, that he would have surely shot us, to help preserve his job, if not for that Israeli's kindness to his mother.

Uganda gained independence from Britain in 1962, maintaining its Commonwealth membership. This was during the time that we were in the country and things were heating up all around us here, as it had happened in Kenya.

A few years after we had left the area and Africa, in 1966, following a power struggle between the Obote-led government and King Muteesa, the United People's Congress dominated Parliament changed the constitution and removed the ceremonial president and vice president. In 1967, a new constitution proclaimed Uganda a republic and abolished the traditional kingdoms. Without first calling elections, Obote was declared the executive President.

During our travels we came upon many beautiful sights. This banana carrier was one of them!

Then, four years later, after a military coup in 1971, Obote was deposed from power and the dictator Idi Amin seized control of the country. Amin ruled Uganda with the military for the next eight years and carried out mass killings within the country to maintain his rule. An estimated 300,000 Ugandans lost their lives at the hands of his regime, many of them in the north, which he associated with Obote's loyalists.

Aside from his brutalities, he forcibly removed the entrepreneurial South Asian minority from Uganda, which left the country's economy in ruins. Amins' atrocities were graphically accounted in the 1977 book, A State of Blood, written by a former minister after he ran out of the country. As mentioned previously; when Arabs from Israeli territories hijacked a passenger plane and had it land in Entebbe, Israeli Defense Forces pulled off a true heroic mission by flying in and freeing all of the passengers. Amin allowed the Arabs total freedom to act as terrorists, which was they were and Amins nose was bloodied by the Israeli's. He was shown up for the buffoon that he was. I believe that helped end his terror reign. He also had an Israeli grandmother who had to be hospitalized just before the Israeli's came in to free the hostages, murdered!

Amin's reign was ended after the Uganda-Tanzania War in 1979, in which Tanzanian forces aided by Ugandan exiles invaded Uganda. This occurred after the so-called "bush war" by the National Resistance Army (NRA) operating under the leadership of the current president, Yoweri Museveni, and various rebel groups, including the Federal Democratic Movement of Andrew Kayiira, and another belonging to John Nkwaanga.

Museveni has been in power since 1986. In the mid- to late 1990s, he was lauded by the West as part of a new generation of African leaders. As president, he has led Uganda in involvement in the civil war in the Democratic Republic of Congo (DRC) and other conflicts in the Great Lakes region. He has struggled for years in the civil war against the Lord's Resistance Army, which has been guilty of numerous crimes against humanity, including child slavery and mass murder. Conflict in northern Uganda has killed untold thousands and displaced millions.

CHAPTER FIVE

UGANDA THROUGH RUWANDA AND BURUNDI TO THE CONGO

After our near tragic encounter at the Congo, Uganda border, we were forced to leave the next morning for a more southern border, some 300-miles out of our way. We drove at an average 20-mile per hour, it was a very long, hot and dusty road towards Rwanda and its border with the Congo. I had to change the cotter pins on the front end linkage about every 50 miles. We did not have spare cotter pins, so we used diaper safety pins, two to each of the connector rods. We were to use over 150 safety pins,(Africa on a Pin & A Prayer) before our vehicle trip was over-the back of my British bush jacket was always brown and dusty!

It could have been an easy border crossing on the Ugandan border with the Congo, but nothing we did in Africa was easy. We began to drive south to the countries of Rwanda, and Burundi, (formerly known as Rwanda, and Urundi). We traveled from a British left-side of the road, to a French, right-side of the road traffic pattern, the same pattern used in the United States.

We pulled into the city of Goma, today with a population of a million people, 50-years ago, maybe 200,000. We headed for the western border area with the Congo, a country, the size of Western Europe that has been at near continuous war between rebels with a communist bent or bandits just out for themselves alone. For the past 60-years, there has almost always been fighting against and for whatever military, representing the mainly corrupt government brought in, by nearly legitimate voting. Today, there is now a spillover of fighting from the Congo of their past two year war into Rwanda. The mostly worthless U.N. is there, and taking sides-what a miserable mess, again and again!

This is a view of a large village outside of Goma, the Capital of Rwanda. All roofs were made of grass and thatch. Thousands were slaughtered here during the Hutu, Tutsi debacle during the Clinton administration. In all more than a half million were murdered in Rwanda.

The people of Rwanda spoke, and were highly influenced and controlled by the French. The food was passable; lots of banana, beans, and rice. Hot sauces were mainly curries. The people (Hutu and Tutsi) were generally very arrogant. The Hutu were the nastiest of all! This stands as a permanent memory to my trip through Rwanda. (Footnote: I was not surprised at the debacle that was the tragedy of at least a million Rwandans killed by their own countrymen. The two tribes involved were Hutu and Tutsi the Hutu killed some 500 thousand Watusi, men, women and children, brutally beheaded and chopped up with machetes). The enmity that existed between sworn enemies erupted into wholesale bloodshed in a reverse coup. These people have killed each other off, each time the slightest excuse surfaced, since the tribes were educated to the white man's ways by religious invasions of their country for the past 150 years. Missionaries did more harm to Africa with proselytizing to a people who believed in animism, prayed to rocks and trees and died young from all the diseases of mankind, down through the ages). Here we were rebuffed by border guards who would not let us into the Congo, but this time we did not try to smash through the barriers as we had in Uganda, for we were sure in Rwanda, they would have shot us dead without a second thought.

We left, passed through the Burundi border and with little fanfare, we continued on to the extremely poor, nearby country of Burundi. Upon entering the country of Burundi, we headed for the Capitol, Usumbura. The buildings and the people really looked rundown and sadly shabby. Poverty seemed to hang over this country like a plague of locusts blotting out the sun. We had set up camp for the night, (our sleeping bags under our Land Rover) on a town square area, across from the Post Office. We believed it to be a safer place to overnight. However, when members of the local constabulary showed up, they warned us that we would possibly never wake up in the morning, as thieves and killers roamed the streets at night and we would be easy victims. So they suggested we go to prison. What they had in mind was that we would go through the locked gates of their city prison and camp out safe and sound for the night on the lawn near the gates. We took them up on their kind offer. We drove through the gates and inmates hanging their arms out of the bars in their cells began cat-calling, making lewd gestures and generally yelling and laughing at us. The novelty soon wore off for them and things quieted down. It was dark, and we crawled into our sleeping bags after dousing ourselves with garlic oil for the night. But, this did not protect us for what happened in the middle of the night. We had parked very close to the downspouts of the 4-story jail, and a torrential rain washed down and under our vehicle literally washing our sleeping bags and us out from under the vehicle. Totally awake and freaked out, we stood there in the darkness soaking wet and stunned to our cores. The next day, we were let out through the gate and after thanking our host police types, we found a sunny spot in the middle of Usumburu, the Capitol of Burundi,(today called Bujumbura) to begin drying out our clothes and sleeping bags. Sneak thieves showed up and we were robbed. They took only the travelers checks out of Gene's bag, not the bag and our passports. That was a close call. We knew we could get our funds back, but it would take a long wait in this part of the world.

These local officials let us into the prison yard for our protection. They were very nice to us after we had been robbed.

While at the post office and after making the necessary arrangements to recover our funds, we met Dr. Jim Johnson. He was a medical, Protestant religious missionary from Indiana on a four year stint at developing and running a medical clinic in the hinterlands of Burundi. He offered us a place to stay and meals for a week at his clinic while we waited for our lost funds to be replaced. His only stipulation was that Gene could assist his wife when she made her rounds of the some 5000 inhabitants of the large village they were set up in. Additionally, I could act as his operating nurse! Talk about being short-handed! What a week it was for both Gene and I.

Dr. Johnson's wife took us to villages in the Usumburu area to meet local residents and dignitaries anxious to meet us. The drums and jungle telegraph told everyone we were in the area. People were extremely curious and friendly!

Before I had left for Israel, the entire preceding year, my mother offered to pay for medical school for me. She wanted me to become a doctor. What mothers does not want their child to be anything else? I promised her I'd think about it and when I returned I would go to a University (which I did, eventually) and take courses that could lead me on the road to becoming a physician. So when Doc Johnson asked me to assist him in a goiter operation, I told him sure. After all, I gutted many fish in my life, so how hard would it be for me to help him handle the swabbing of blood, the handing of surgeon tools to him, etc. Well, this swollen and infected goiter on the women's neck was a real mess of blood and fluids. It was frankly, horrible-nothing like cleaning a clean, healthy fish. The odors were horrendous, the sight of this bug-eyed lady laid out on the operating table was not what I was really up to at that time. Fortunately, the operation was a success, I was as happy it was over, as the woman was. Later on after lunch, Doc Johnson told me he had 6 different women giving birth that day. He asked me to handle a couple of them. Oy! I did! Fortunately, there were no breached births in my horoscope that day. One girl, about 14-years old literally popped the baby out almost like a cork exploding out of bottle of Champagne. The woman had a boy; I named him in my mind and under my breath "Ugulu" for "Ugly as hell!" I swear the little guy had a big penis, a little; just born, miss-shaped head, and because he was just born and I had never witnessed, nor had anything in my memory bank remotely to go on, and I didn't even have to slap his behind to begin letting him clear his tiny lungs, I felt all was a success. I found that the younger the females, the easier births that they had. The second birth of the day was even weirder for me. The woman was in her early 20's and this was her 4th birth. I had to assist a bit, but when the baby slid out into a towel held by a woman helper, the woman grabbed the umbilical cord and wouldn't let me cut it. She bit it off herself! I sure was growing up at Doc Johnsons clinic. Later on in the day, I did have a terrific experience, not to say being involved with birthing is not. I met Nickie!

Dr. Jim Johnson had a delightful, 12-year old daughter named Nickie. She spoke the local language; Lingalese after just one year in Burundi and when she found out I loved to fish, she made a point to help me sneak away to do just that. She was a true young adventuress. I could now call her the only little sister I ever had. Mischievous, bright, wildly animated -whoever eventually married her when she grew up, was a very lucky man to find her. Her mother Kathy was a sweet, smart, hard working lady who asked me to send her a book on Calligraphy when I returned home to USA. Much later on, I did just that! I have not heard from them now, for many decades, I hope they are living a happy healthy life. They were spectacular human beings, to be emulated for a better world today!

On my second evening at the clinic, I saw the big communal village bonfire and dancing bodies silhouetted in the glow. I walked over to where the village Witch Doctor, who was performing exorcisms of various and sundry demons. He regaled the crowd of villagers with incantations as he wowed them with various powders that he threw into the fire. They flared into various colors that were to represent the different demons that he was telling the crowd he was excising. Little Nickie acted as my interpreter and told me about everything that was going on. It was fascinating to see the obvious belief and seeming comprehension of the superstitions and legends concerning evil and good witches and omens that the villagers were being harangued about, and as it all was portrayed that night, in the wide-eyed villagers faces. Animism was the original religion of these peoples of Africa and that belief, seemed to always be just under the surface, as that fantasy materialized right over the top of many, in their newer beliefs in the Christian doctrines. Kathy asked us if we wanted to visit a nearby village. She had gotten word that the village leader wanted to throw a dinner party for us. We went into this town and I felt like a rock star would have. Seems all the young men and women wanted to meet and shake our hands. Then a fellow of about 25-years of age showed up in a black suit, white shirt and a purple tie. He was to be our host in this village. He invited us to come into his home to meet his cousins. He had several women cousins as he called them. Turned out they were his wives, all four of them that he called his cousins. Seemed there was taboo to some extent for men to have so many wives. More like calling them all his wives would be like bragging and showing his good fortune and money off. All were very cordial and one of his wives was told to go get the chicken that would be our meal for the evening. I peered out the window and watched this girl chase a rooster, a scrawny example of a fowl as I had ever seen. She ran all around with a hatchet running up and down the road chasing this bird. Finally, exhausted the girl and the chicken she grabbed it by the neck, laid it over a stump and began the process of making it the featured item on the menu that night. Feathers were flying in the breeze and eventually I did smell the distinct odor of roasted chicken. The rooster was a tough bird, I believe it would never have been killed if we had not been coming for dinner, but it seemed that was all they had that night that was fresh.

There were vegetables; yams, carrots, some sort of beans and rice, toasted bread, and the rooster I actually traveled with garlic cloves in my pocket and would instantly slice up some to add to every meal I ate. However, I knew I would be disrespectful to doctor my dish in front of the family and cook. Fortunately, the veggies had some roasted garlic. I was happy about that. However, the meat was so tough I had a very hard time chewing it enough to swallow it. The awaiting dogs enjoyed my instant leftovers under the table. We drank passion fruit juice, and coconut water. I did belch quite a lot and smiles were seen all around, even though I couldn't pass gas from the other end of my starving body, the belches worked just fine! After being asked a thousand questions in French from our host, we left with Kathy after chewing some sugar cane and having real mint tea. We enjoyed our time in this little burgh and were meant to feel right at home there. We went back at the village with grass roofs, Kathy and Bob Johnson's clinic village, Kathy told us about some interesting facts about what goes on in the village on a socio/psychological front. She mentioned that there was an albino young man and his pure white skin was a terrible burden to him and his family. He was looked at as a freak of nature and treated with a certain unwanted respect. Because of him being pure white, he was off limits to everyone in the village socially. He was feared as perhaps a witch and he had a very short lifespan. Kathy said that albinos in her experience in Africa never quite make their 20th birthday. They die of Melanoma cancer, having no resistance to the suns destructive radiation on the skin. Up to date on albinism; the following report was introduced from Tanzanian Governmental records in 2013: According to a March 2013 news report, there has been an increase in attacks on people with albinism. Four attacks occurred in 2013 between 31

January and 15 February. Their body parts, which can sell for a total of US $75,000, are used in witchcraft. Not much has changed since visiting and living in Africa over 52 years ago. Not much has changed at all!

A BIT ABOUT THE COUNTRY OF BURUNDI

"Burundi is a landlocked small nation in Africa. Burundi is a part of the western extension of the East African Rift. The country lies on a rolling plateau, in the center of Africa. The source of the Nile River is in Bururi province, and is linked from Lake Victoria. Lake Victoria is also an important water source. It serves as a fork to the Kagera River. Another major lake is Lake Tanganyika, located in much of Burundi's southwestern corner. This is a country of an estimated population of 10,557,259 people. Today, most of these people are Catholic and Burundi is one of the world's poorest countries, owing in part to its landlocked geography, poor legal system, lack of economic freedom, lack of access to education, and the proliferation of HIV/AIDS. When we traveled in Africa in 1963-64, we had never heard of HIV/AIDS, if we had, I never would have gone there. Approximately 80% of Burundi's population lives in poverty. Famines and food shortages have occurred throughout Burundi, most notably in the 20th century, according to the World Food Program, 56.8% of children under age five suffer from chronic malnutrition. One scientific study of 178 nations rated Burundi's population as having the lowest satisfaction with life in the world. As a result of poverty, Burundi is dependent on foreign aid. Wikipedia information-October-2013

Burundi's lands are mostly agricultural or pasture. Settlement by rural populations has led to deforestation, soil erosion and habitat loss. Deforestation of the entire country is almost completely due to overpopulation, with a mere 230 square miles remaining and an ongoing loss of about 9% per annum. Wherever we drove, it was a dusty, vacant land. There are two national parks, Kibira National Park to the northwest (a small region of rain forest, adjacent to Nyungwe Forest National Park in Rwanda), Ruvubu National Park to the northeast (along the Rurubu River, also known as Ruvubu or Ruvuvu). Both were established in 1982 to conserve wildlife populations. People are so poor, that there are more rangers in these parks than animals to protect the remnants of a once thriving wildlife population, now decimated by their use as food for the masses.

Many Burundians have migrated to other countries as a result of the civil war. In 2006, the United States accepted approximately 10,000 Burundian refugees. Think about it; Burundian women have over 6-children each. Do the math! Burundi has the fifth highest total fertility rate in the world, at 6.08 children born. (2012 estimates)

CHAPTER SIX

TRAVELING TO KIGALI, THE FUEL STATION INCIDENT, THE PYGMIES

Eventually we did find a border crossing at the Rwanda/Burundi border area. Because the border guards couldn't afford to feed and care for traveling wayfarers that crossed the border, they wished to get them rides by anyone with transportation going or coming in either direction, just so they could be rid of the burden. We did have a condition imposed on us in passing through the border, which included a bribe, was that, we had to transport a passenger to his village. The man we were saddled with used elephant dung in his hair, much the same way a western greaser would do his pompadour in the 1950s. Unfortunately, the stench of the feces was intolerable, even though we were coated with garlic. We were used to the smell of garlic, compared to pachyderm dung, but it did nothing to help mask the malodorous conditions. He sat just behind us on top of our belongings, and we could not communicate with him at all.

We joked with him in sign language, and in every way we thought he might understand. He remained aloof and stiff, and we were sure he was miffed at us not being able to speak his Lingala language (Lingalese was the official Congolese language, in the part of the Congo we were entering, at least). We spoke some Swahili, which we learned in Kenya and Uganda, but he didn't seem to understand that either. Finally, with heaven's mercy, he motioned to us to pull off the road so he could relieve himself, and we were thankful of this, since the smell had given us a headache, and even some stomach distress. As he moved towards the bushes we made a hasty retreat, and bid our luckless friend adieu.

I watched in my mirror, as he raced out to the road, standing there peering after us with a puzzled look on his face. I felt sorry about our leaving him, but the smell still permeated our vehicle, and our nostrils, so our regrets turned into thankfulness.

Checkpoint in Congo. Gene went out to offer some cigarettes to these Government soldiers at a checkpoint. It was good that Gene was fluent in French! It took me 2-months to be elementary fluent in French (enough to get by with).

After a while we began itching, and realized that he had left us another present; fleas. The garlic had worn off that first day in the Congo, from sitting and sweating so long. I personally remedied the situation by squeezing a sufficient amount of raw garlic juice from a clove, applying it to my buttocks and legs just to make sure we chased away every bug possible; bugs left by our previous walking pariah, our unwanted, forced upon us, guest.

I had learned long before I arrived in Africa that the shortest route between two points traveled, or on paper was a straight line. In Africa there are no straight lines or roads. Most of the terrain in Africa consisted of serpentine roads and circuitous ways up and down the countryside. A trek through this land was then, and I understand full well now, a trip through pre-history for anyone from the west. Things in the west have changed rapidly, socially, the industrial revolution and of course the biggest change of all; electronic communications with the internet, but in Africa with the exception of the diamond, religious missionary and rubber business interests, few things have changed except for the horror of AIDS. People that are used to very fast changes in the relativity of the new worlds terms and times would be flabbergasted by the actual snail-like pace of change in Africa. People in Africa, not the citified ones, do things, (crafts, building their dwellings, doing anything beyond attending to the daily natural personal hygiene needs) they do their wash in streams and gather brush and branches for cooking fires, they brush their teeth with chewed and crushed branch ends, the way they have done for untold centuries. Africans, those that have not become accustomed to the white man's ways, still do things one at a time, often with pride and high utility. Because time is not money to most of these peoples, a hand carved knife may take days or weeks to craft and speed is not part of the criteria for its fashioning. Quality, not quantity would seem to describe the craftsman's philosophy in the hinterlands of Africa.

When we traded for such things as hand-made knives and finger pianos, or spears or any item an African makes for himself or others of his tribe, manufactured products from the west, such as razor blades, shiny nail clippers or cigarettes was what they wanted for exchange. Modern manufactured items such as these that may as well have been made by aliens from another planet were perfect barter and trade item products. For the Africans, it was future-shock, they were delighted with chromium products and for us their hand crafted things were museum quality items that we would also be treating as priceless. I remember seeing this trade as realistic and fair, even though on cursory notice through western eyes and perspective it would seem the Africans were the ones being taken advantage of, they did and would certainly feel the same way about their good fortune. After all, they looked at the transactions from their own perspective. They could make another mask, knife, spear, monkey strap and bow and arrow set out of the natural free material around them. They were sure that the white man's technology would be very difficult, if not impossible to reproduce even for the traders from a land of the future. They were correct, even us modern guys couldn't make those items without being schooled in industrial arts. And, we delivered these items from countries and areas they could not even hope to travel to.

I made this serpentine road shot in Congo as we climbed up and down many hills and mountains on our way to Stanleyville. We were very fortunate to have a 4-wheel, sure-footed, trustworthy vehicle for all the rutted curves up and down some very steep grades.

Africa was not just a place. It was a state of mind. Everywhere we looked, there were things to marvel at. From the style and shapes of African homes and buildings to the dress and customs of these peoples from a lush land, nourished by an equatorial sun and heavy rainy seasons, to the diversity of a people that Thomas Leaky was sure are the ancient ancestors of the birth of Homo Erectus, or the first man-like man who stood erect.

Traveling through Africa and experiencing its diverse wildlife, I had no doubt why anyone would not think that this place perhaps was where the concept of the Garden of Eden had come from. Every fruit known to man grows somewhere in Africa, almost every wild animal including the largest land animal the pachyderm and the smallest the Madagascar shrew is indigenous to this continent and its Indian Ocean environs. There are over 500 different types of snakes, fifty thousand kinds of insects, hundreds of varieties of fish, reptiles and amphibians inhabit the waters, lands and jungles of Africa, not to mention the over 100 or more different mammalian species that dot the plains, inhabit the trees with over 600 species of birds, countless kinds of trees and plants as well as the throwback from the dinosaur age the crocodile. These crocodiles yearly account for hundreds of deaths. People get too close to them as they wash their clothes, take baths and fish in the rivers and lakes and become food for many of these crocodiles. Many crocs reach in access of 20 feet in length and a ton in weight. There are hundreds of butterflies and moth varieties besides the other aforementioned insect numbers, dozens of leech and worm types and you can meet many of them by just taking a swim in any still water pool, lake or river. Just walking under a tree or brushing against a bush or tall grasses also lets leeches, ticks and sundry critters take a bite out of you. We met a few of all of them, at one time or another. My garlic odor kept them off me, but not off of Gene.

Gene and I traveled through a land of giant bamboo, some bamboo trunks were as big around as a barrel. The trees seemed to reach the clouds; many of these trees nearly did in the highlands of Kisangani National Park. We took in the fragrance of exotic aromas from wildflowers and craned our necks to view the orchids high in the tree boughs. We passed so many waterfalls and natural sights, noticed so many fragrances, all our senses were constantly being bombarded with new, exciting; some just plain scary things (like a few of the giant spider webs that hung between bushes and trees. To relieve yourself, you always had to pay attention to your surroundings) that we were on an "info-processing overload" much of the time.

A view through the windshield of our rover and tire on hood of a decent dirt road we traveled in the Congo, most roads were not so flat. After every rain you had to watch out or nearly drown your rig sometimes.

We traveled down a dusty, sometimes muddy road; filled with ruts and high, untamed grasses in the roads center, where tires rarely tread. In the twilight of a late African afternoon we spied a small village off in the distance, and after not seeing another human for days, we decided to stop and visit with the villagers and possibly trade for some fresh fruit, and perhaps a chicken dinner. As we got closer to the outskirts of the village, we saw what we expected were the inhabitants peering through the window openings in their huts. Throughout our visits to villages in the east and central African nations, we'd grown accustomed to the children running out to greet us. However, when we pulled into the village, there were no children or people.

Suddenly, we became aware that what peered out at us was not human. What lived in these huts were baboons. Not just your average plains baboons mind you, but street and town smart ones. Further down that road towards Stanleyville in the Congo, we met other Bantu people who explained the strange experience we had with this occurrence. To our astonishment, we learned that the people in the village died out and the survivors fled from the raging yellow fever epidemic, so when the people left, the baboons moved in to take their place. Yes, we were concerned about this when we found out about the disease factor, but we never went near the buildings thanks to the fact that we knew that some baboons were definitely meat eaters and we had no guns with us.

We saw things in The Congo in the fields of science, medicine, and philosophy that in terms of our western religion and life-experiences could not be explained. One example of many with which we experienced, is the time we stayed overnight in a village with no lights, and no concept of electricity. Oil lamps, like in the days of old, were normal, and we sat around a large fire, while the shaman of the village, called on the good spirits to come forth, and the malevolent ones to stay away. This ritual entailed powders to be thrown into the fire, causing flash points, which the shaman was able to attribute to spirit movement and signs from their gods. The people believed in the show and it was hard for me and Gene, with all the palm wine we imbibed, not to feel the same way at the time.

I'm reminded of a time just a few days after our passing up over and through the aforementioned rain forest, when we found a gas station and an attendant with a flying horse insignia on his cap who assured us he had fuel and plenty of it. We were delighted, due to the fact that we did not like to dip into our emergency 55-gallon drum; we carried in the rear of the rover, unless we absolutely had to. The reason for this was for the obvious reason that fuel was so scarce in the

Congo. We fueled up, gas was 12-cents per gallon, and we headed out and towards the Ruwenzori Game Park, on our way ultimately, towards the Leopoldville, capitol in the Congo. One mile out of town our rover sputtered and died. We checked the engine, all was fine, however our fuel line filter and glass bowl on the carburetor was obviously filled with water. I sent a shot glass on a string down into our under- the-seat gas tank. Low and behold, we came up with straight, water. The attendant had pumped water into our tank. We were a bit upset, especially due to the fact that here we were in the heat of tropical sun with no serviceable vehicle, no weapon (except my ever present double edged sword) and the major gut feeling, that we had been had. Under the vehicle there was a petcock that was rust-frozen shut. We did not want to break open the fitting and have a leaking gas tank. So we used the shot glass to the highest and best use, under the circumstances. If you ever had to empty a barrel with a thimble you would have approximated our feeling and predicament, which lasted for a very long time, exacerbated by a 110-degree temperature. We were sweating so heavily, that our eyes were in constant tears from our brows mini waterfall. We finally accomplished cleaning out our carburetor, tank, and fuel line of water (we wished our vehicle was a steam engine from the beginning to the end of that ordeal) and then filled our tank from the aforementioned, standby, 55-gallon reserve barrel. Our rover leaped to life, with the proper blood in her veins and we drove back, the one-mile to the service station. There were many men milling around the tanks, talking to the attendant or owner or both and when we explained to him what happened, which was a bad 6 hours after we had left him in the morning, he shrugged his shoulders and refused any relief for us, including any payback. We did not argue the point, due to the fact that the law was as-you-found-it, in the Congo. White was not right at the time, especially Americans in this newly Chinese communist run, co-dictatorship. We decided to move on, yet I mentally blew up the place using my own gasoline many times over the next several days. I believe however, to this day, that the attendant at the station may not have known the difference between fuel and water, and any attempt to teach him by us, would have resulted in failure at that time. In the 1960's most people that we met in the Congo believed in Animistic Gods. Their Gods were in the rocks and trees and anywhere they thought, or were taught they were. We left the fueling station feeling lucky that the attendant did not try to clean our windshield.

On another day in our travels as the sun began kissing the tree tops and the jungle was preparing to rest, (actually, the jungle never completely rests, the day creatures of the canopy, ground and waters shift off and make way for the night denizens to take over) we were too!

We eventually came upon a village in the Kigali rain forest. We arrived late one evening after driving for far too long, although not very far. On our way to this area of the Congo, we had to climb a very steep mountain. This in itself was an adventure. We arrived to the bottom of the mountain road and witnessed more than 60 trucks and other vehicles all camped out on the side of the road, there were drivers cooking out over bamboo fires and then we saw the sign! A big sign in French, stating that the road was a one way, extremely narrow and as such there was a schedule. The schedule was that the day we arrived for 24-hours was down hill only, the following day as it turned out was the uphill day. So we camped out waiting for the next day road opening for all of us camped out at the bottom of the mountain. As we spoke French we chatted with some of the drivers and as this country was on a sleep and crawl basis, they didn't seem to mind the one day delay at all. We woke very early and in time to line up to head up the mountain. A whistle was blown by a fellow wearing a Sinclair Oil and gas hat sideways. The procession (we were 2nd in line), proceeded up the mountain.

We headed up the mountains at an eight degree grade in the Kigali National Forest and the Mafuga Forest with inches to spare from a fast fall from heaven to hell on the rut busted road. Our 1955 Land Rover crept at a speed just shy of 4-mph. We were loaded with camping gear, a sleeping bag each, lots of garlic as "bug-off and out", a canvas bag full of pond water, laced with Halazone tablets for keeping the live bugs out of our guts, hung over our exterior radiator cap as we traveled. The water evaporation off the bag as the air hit it at 5 or 10 miles per hour kept the water at least tepid instead of hot. But no, that did not work since most places up that mountain were slow going. We were going just 2-miles per hour. I felt we were lucky as the vehicle first in line was in reasonably decent shape. So, I thought that perhaps he wouldn't breakdown and hold us and the line of other 60 or more vehicles behind us up.

Then, after driving for at least a half- hour uphill, here came a big truck coming down the mountain on our so-called regulated road schedule. Oh, my G-D, this was a nightmare. The driver of the downhill truck insisted we all had to back up because he could not go in reverse back up the hill. If it wasn't so dangerous and dumb we probably could have laughed this episode off, but it definitely was not funny. Out came the machetes, I stood behind our Land Rover and let the driver in front and the ones behind us take charge of the situation. To this day, I don't really know how this ended without bloodshed. The upshot was the guy and his co-pilot had to literally pickax against the hill, fill in a rain rut and move over to let us up the mountain. It took 3-hours and the drop was totally precarious; one wrong move and whoever went off that road was a goner. Our vehicle barely made it around the frame of a long ago destroyed mirror on that truck; I could only guess how well the big trucks following us up the mountain would fare? When we arrived at the top of the mountain there were dozens of trucks filled with lumber products and assorted agricultural goods waiting as we had for their turn to head down the mountain. A couple of the men told us they warned that driver stuck down along the narrow road not to go, but he didn't listen. This of course wasn't anything new. No matter where you went, or what you did, things always seemed to go willy nilly at the whim of so many adamant, mostly uneducated, very head-strong people, half of whom were either high on Bangui or local potato beer.

We headed along the ridge of the mountain and eventually took a road that seemed to be rarely used on our way towards our destination which was to find the Pygmies of the Ituri Rainforest. The first evening, after our climb up that mountain, we camped out in the shadows of a village that we saw as we turned a curve in the road. We only saw the village due to their campfires glow that illuminated the outlines of their huts. The villager's campfires were tended and burned all night out of fear of the unknown. Additionally the fear of the known such as leopards that growled and prowled, snakes, and in this part of the world, witches were real, and malevolent spirits that were believed in by all the jungle peoples. We watched the villagers from a distance peering at us from the edge of their dwelling huts seen by the light of their fires. We were not afraid ourselves, as we had grown accustomed to the fact that bush villagers and peoples in the hinterlands of Africa were very friendly and not at all like the images we had come to know in Tarzan movies and other extremely phony Hollywood productions. Only when we were in, or near cities where the white man's influence was heavy and well-remembered, did we have to be concerned with our safety and our belongings. However, we really slept with one eye open that night because these were the first native peoples we had seen in a long time and could not be totally at ease until the next day when the light of dawn would reassure both us and these people that we mutually meant each other no harm. All fear was dispelled upon waking to a lucidly beautiful sight of children bearing fruit as a friendly gesture for our breakfast. Wide-eyed children all, we were sure that their parents sent them as an advance guard to check us out, before the adults would dare make contact with us. They had no problem, as we didn't. They were very friendly and quite curious about our trip and reason for sleeping under our Land Rover, the ultimate camping adventure of my life. We traded a bit with them, some razor blades and cigarettes for carved figurines and more papaya, guava and bananas for our later consumption. We always tried to plan ahead a bit on food and water, for we never knew when we would be fortuitous enough to find food again. There were no 7 11's, fast food or farmers markets on the majority of this trip, and the very few fuel stations that we found were usually out of fuel and oil anyway. We headed out as early as we could see the road ahead, without having to rely on our headlights.

Even at that time in 1962-63 we realized we were in a different world and paradigm, both we from the future, and they from the past; then for a moment in real- time our lives intersected with theirs. Each of us had our own view of life, and all it meant to them, and for us. This adventure was never boring; it was always exhilarating to me. Every bend in the road, every stop to take a break and stretch from sitting and bouncing along on roads that were really only wide dirt and rut-filled paths. The sights and aromas, the sounds of insects and the frogs, jungle cats and monkeys, even the breezes that rustled the bamboo forests causing a certain clacking noise was different, interesting and exciting!

CHAPTER SEVEN

RELIGIOUS MONKS, PYGMY ADVENTURE IN ITURI RAIN FOREST

On the way into the Congo we had stopped at a Greek Orthodox Monastery, whose monks invited us to stay for a few days. While we were there, we gave a few guest lectures to students in their school. The monasteries monks developed the school for youngsters in the surrounding areas of Burundi. The Monks spoke Greek, English, French and Lingalese. They had been teaching English to their "boys" at their school. They wanted us to talk about our trip and America to them.

The monastery was like a medieval fortress of ancient times, with its early Greek revival architecture, balustrades, and ionic columns, beautiful gardens, and fountains. You could feel the great love and dedication in its crafting. Gene and I both felt the specialness of these Monks; they were truly devoted men, who with their simplified stress free lives, were making a lifelong statement with their piety and endless devotion to their maker. Here they stayed all their days teaching, keeping gardens and farm animals, so that the lives of the people they desired to help would and could lead healthier, more educationally expanded, and better existences. We were touched by their unending kindness, and we felt a thoroughly peaceful friendship with these kindred souls.

We played billiards on a table that looked like it had come from the medieval period, with its lions faced embossments, carved griffins, and beast table legs, who knows, perhaps it did. Our meals were simple, consisting of bread, beef, and nourishing vegetables, and the way everyone ate and talked together, led to a conviviality that has since been unmatched.

They worked their own vineyards and made their own wine. Also, all their produce and foods were grown on the monastery grounds. Having such profuse food gardens enabled them to have a learning center for their students of agriculture and animal husbandry. The Monks were experimenting with cross-breeding of a couple of different antelopes. They were attempting to develop a group of animals that could take the place of beef cattle in the area. The antelopes were used to their environment and could browse in brush and grasses that cows could not. The antelopes were also more resistant to various diseases and water borne and airborne pests. The monks provided a bright light in an age, and area of darkness where the shaman's spirits, ghosts, and deities played a role in keeping ignorance at a level that made progress in important areas, such as health, and education next to impossible. At least these monks of the Greek Orthodox Church were a bastion, and a repository of learning. That gave these people some choice out of a society which had the most crooked politicians and public servants, who were at least obvious about it, compared to some societies of our world. It appeared normal to us that it was; "get all you can for yourself, if you can and the hell with everyone else." It was taken to a fine art, and was most obvious when the starving people of Africa received aid from American liberty ships that President Kennedy authorized in 1962. These ships were summarily intercepted by officials of the African nations and sold at a great and crime ridden profit to anyone who could afford it. "Let the starving people be dammed", appeared to be their motto.

At the Monastery and previously on the road in Tanganyika we met Peace Corps volunteers. Basically, they said that whatever they tried to do in that country to help the lives of the poor was usually meaningless, due to the fact that they got little if any support from local officials that were assigned to help them in this regard. With the exception of these Peace Corp volunteers experiencing a new culture and environment, they felt they were wasting their time in the Peace Corps, in Africa. We met two young women hitch-hiking back to the village that they were staying and working in. They said that they were tasked to put in water wells and a rudimentary sewer system. I told the gals to keep it simple by building two-hole outhouses. They said they had money to do much more than outhouses, but Gene told them if they "keep it simple, they would come." They laughed, threw back their heads, with pony tails whipping back and forth, reminding me of the sweet damsels that I had left in the Israel and the U.S. Of course tried to agree, but they came to do a job, had money to do it and they had their own ideas. One of them was blond, I worried about her. She definitely was in over her head with her ditsy attitude, that everyone liked her there-yes, sure the crease in her pants and the bumps on her chest! We had stopped to talk to them and asked them if they didn't think they were taking a big chance, even being in the country at this time? They answered that so far no one had bothered them and the people were so nice and friendly. So far was luck, just luck I told them. They can't live on luck. We warned them that "they could be eaten as their sweet meat will attract both leopards and cannibals. They laughed at us and went on their way refusing a ride to their village. We never did hear about them again, but we did hear some women had been raped and murdered in the area, and they were Peace Corps volunteers. Whoever sent them to this part of Africa should have been hung!

Traveling on and into to the Congo, we drove through areas that showed the great influence that the Belgians had on the nation. Every city we went to, that was close to the Congo River, we found the architecture to mirror the French provincial designs of Belgium and France. Rococo architecture was also an obvious indicator of the mix of European peoples that once heavily inhabited and exploited the peoples and natural resources of this very fertile land. First the Portuguese, then Spaniards, the French, the British, and finally the Belgians ate some of their natural resources. The Dutch were there working the rubber trees, the Italians were looking for oil, and the Church was always mining for souls. Gold was sought, diamonds, wood products. Coming at them when we were there, were the Chinese.

The resentment by the locals towards us was quite obvious, as we traveled through the more built up areas of the Congo. Everywhere we went, the history of the Congo's colonialization made for bitterness that we had to experience. We did not feel this as much as we traveled through the rural areas. The native people, for the most part, were very friendly throughout our journey of the many African nations that we had visited. In a few larger towns that we drove into, we did not feel welcome at all. There were a few times we had to race out of town in front of a small group, or horde of men and women, threatening us with machetes.

We eventually traveled through the mountains of the Ituri rain forest, a forest whose mountains held the famous, mountain gorilla. Here we met our first tribe of pygmies. Yes, they were small in physical stature, but definitely big of heart and warmth of friendliness, a more delightful group of people would be difficult to imagine. They more than made up for the diminutive size, in large doses of their friendly, fun loving, and demonstratively, personable acceptance of us. We were to learn that they were frightened by any strangers, because they had been mistreated, and in many cases had become the victims of cannibals by both black men, and white men. It appeared that they would be walking down the road, and suddenly be kidnapped by people that not only enslaved them, but ate them as well. Meat was scarce in almost all areas of Africa, and almost any animal was fair game, including man. Another rational thought of by cannibals, was eating of another human gave that person eating of the other flesh and brain the strength and positive attributes of that person. One reason it appeared that the pygmies were taken, was they were smaller, and weaker than their adversaries, yet they were great hunters and because they had no organized vendetta system as other tribes had, they were safe human meat. So, if a pygmy was abducted, the generally more casual attitude of the tribe and its loose knit hierarchy, did not take revenge as readily as other tribes did. So they were easy, and generally safe prey compared to other tribes in the lower and upper hills of the jungle and forests.

For us, we found the pygmies to be the most natural, and closest to nature's people that we ever encountered. They were not devious, they shared everything. They appeared not to have any jealousy about their possessions, nor their women, nor for that matter, anything. They weren't just friendly, they were open, and everything was tit for tat. Your friendship was immediately matched, and far and away surpassed. They fell over themselves to give little gifts, and to offer their women for the night, or time you would spend with them. Whatever your pleasure, the pygmies wished to fulfill it. This was similar to the Eskimos history, of wanting a visitor to have the pleasure, and comfort of sleeping with the head of the household's wife. This was a courtesy, of course. We did not avail ourselves of the pygmy's courtesies; however, we did actively trade with them for their handmade bows and arrows, gourd wine pipes, spears and ivory carvings.

We ate roast snake, bananas and monkey, although we had a hard time with the roast monkey. It looked remarkably like young pygmies, and being brought up in a kosher home, I knew cannibalism was a major sin from the hundreds of commandments of the original ten. No matter how hungry, we never even fantasized about that abomination.

We watched Pygmies hunt with their blowguns for brightly colored birds, monkeys, and a small antelope species-the Dik Dik. They skinned and used the feathers for adornments, and ceremonial garb, then roasted and ate the birds. They used the skins of monkeys for materials to fashion arrow quivers, and small knap sacks, and roasted the monkey. I observed how they dispatched a howler monkey after shooting it with a poisoned tipped dart, by taking the drugged, and dying animal by the tail, and slamming its head against an available tree. They do this so the monkey could not turn and bite them just in case the drug did not fully incapacitate it.

Pygmy women and children the largest of them were not quite 4-foot 5 inches.

I would be remiss in not describing, in detail, an elephant hunt made by the pygmies, to stock up on meat for the entire village. It seemed that we were destined still to get close to elephant dung. In order for us to be able to go along on the hunt, which was to be undertaken by the tribes young savages, we would have to cover up our scent, and yes, you guessed it, we needed to use elephant dung on all our private parts, and of course our hair as well, to mask our human scent. We acquiesced to their friendly chiding demands, and got naked and full of pachyderm dung. We followed behind the group, who had dogs with wooden bells around their necks. The dogs with the bell with wooden clappers trod the path before us, this was done to warn any poisonous snakes of our approach, so they can slither away, and not by chance, offer us what would certainly have been a fatal injection of venom. There were green and black mambas, and a whole variety of poisonous kraits, that we later learned could have killed us in less than a few minutes. Fortunately, on that day none of our party was bitten.

Pygmy dogs with wooden bells. The clacking of the clappers in the wooden bells frightened and warned snakes that something that could harm them were coming their way. So the snakes would sliver away off the paths and the hunters would not get struck.

Off in the distance we heard the unmistakable sound of elephants. The men were armed with spears and machetes, no guns. The group began using hand signals, and we stealthily made our way towards the increasingly noisier sounds of foraging elephants. By a hand signal, everyone stopped and one of the hunters climbed a tree. We thought it would be a better vantage point to see their quarry. However, the real reason became apparently clear when the hunter removed several very light breast feathers from a bird that he had killed. He then proceeded to drop these feathers, and we observed the direction the wind and breezes were blowing from the direction the feathers floated. The hunting party then began to move so as to position itself downwind of the elephants so that the elephants would not be alarmed by our scent, or noise from our movements. We all moved into play like some primeval Neanderthal hunting party. The killing hunter, the hunter with the mark of superiority and chief warrior, took a spear with a very sharp and sturdy blade, and began first walking then crawling towards the unaware herd of animals. He picked out a young cow, which stood at least twelve feet high, and stealthily began his move to sneak up and crawl under her belly, while it peacefully fed on some leaves from a nearby bush. The hunter rolled under the elephant and struck up and at the heart of the great beast. It screamed with the pain, and surprise of its mortal wound, and the herd trumpeted, and rallied to its immediate defense. As quickly as the hunter had struck, he rolled out of the way, and made his way as fast as he could, away from the herd. The mortally wounded animal took off, profusely bleeding from its wound, while a big bull standing guard and trumpeting a warning back in our direction of its displeasure and fear. As the group made off through the forest, we followed at a quick pace, the plan was obvious by then, we would follow until the struck gargantuan bled to death, then wait till the other elephants finally left after trying to protect, and raise its great bulk to life. We would then step in and butcher the beast, and return to the village with the meat festooned with flies, and other insects attracted to the warm and bloody meat.

We followed and passed through a forest that till this day with its giant ferns, and vines, and its huge and colorful butterflies, beetles, and flowers, reminded me of the dioramas of ancient prehistoric forests that I had seen when I was a boy on my trips with my mother to the museum of natural history. The experience which prevailed upon all my senses was astonishing, I felt as if I had truly been blessed with the right to see, and experience the deep dark past, and only special feelings, and difficult terms would be possible to fully convey that time, those hidden places, and sensations. So I must leave this to my reader's imagination for the best possible effect for you to grasp.

We came upon a remarkable scene. The group of elephants fretted over their fallen member, and the scene was very sad for my western eyes. The feeling was that someone of my family was hurt seriously and the entire family tried in vain to help where there was no help possible. I felt for those animals, I recall shedding more than one tear that day. I was there, at the raw edge of humanity, and the experience had me awe struck. I never felt so alive, and close to the wide open nerve of life and death before. Here I was, I mused while waiting along with the hunters for the elephants to depart from their dead family member, in the guts of a savage and strangely beautiful interlude, whose experience was mind boggling, yet so natural as to dispel any doubt that I should be any other happening than as this reality presented to us. Many minutes passed into hours, and finally the last animal abandoned its family member. The hunters fell upon the warm carcass of the elephant, and began slicing great chunks of meat from the animal. The small tusks were cut, sawed, and hammered into submission, out and away from their supreme owner. The tusks would be carved into representations of forest and river animals, such as crocodiles, snakes, small antelope, and monkeys. The trunk was taken off with several hacks of a hunter's machete, to be used in a roast for the hunters, to commemorate their kill, and to also prove their sexual prowess feeding on this appendage, which was considered a great aphrodisiac. Most of the meat was hoisted upon the heads of the hunters, and we began a long trek home. We had ranged several miles from where the original attack was made, we now had to backtrack. The pygmies did this with unerring accuracy. Many hours later we arrived back at camp, having first been met by a contingent of youths, who greeted us well before we reached the village. The men had blown antelope horns, which the pygmies used upon entrance to the village. Everyone was dancing to the beat of a successful and safe return from the hunt. We learned later that sometimes lions or leopards, so excited by the smell of fresh elephant meat, would attack the returning huntsmen, and so just getting home from a trip deep into the woods was an important occurrence, and accomplishment worth partying over. Actually any occurrence that seemed to work out in favor of the tribe and the majority of its members was cause for a celebration.

The Pygmy adults sat around a large fire at night, and smoked hashish; a sort of Bangui through wine filled gourds, whose stems were dry stems of the plants, and whose gourd areas were hollowed out. A baked clay bowl was inserted into a hole on the top of the gourd. In this vessel was poured palm wine, and in the bowl the hashish embers glowed. The smoke mixed with the alcoholic spirits, then the potent heady mixture was inhaled deeply, absolutely stunning the senses. I felt that I belonged in that jungle forest after just two puffs of this concoction, and I too saw the night spirits dancing before my drug effected, and inflicted eyes. The world turned very simple, as I recall, and I realized now why these pygmies are still exactly the same way now as they were in the millennium, and haven't progressed a lick, except for some trade items haphazardly acquired by the infrequent visitors to their realm. And just maybe, that's a good thing for them? After that first night, all I wanted to do from then on was play, and just work hard enough to acquire my next meal, and look no further than one day, or one moment at a time. Then reality set in, we had to move on. So in a few days, we bid farewell to our new friends, who had an average life expectancy of 35-years of age, (a 60-year old was ancient) and who we will never see again, but of whom we will never forget. Disease and malnutrition continues to take its toll on the Congolese people and so unfortunately, it has been this way for far too many decades. The Pygmies then, as they are more so now, on their way to extinction as more and more of the traditional forests are being stripped for natural resources by extremely greedy peoples. However, today when a gorilla is poached, there is genuine grief as this big ape has found the heart-strings of many Congolese, who believe that these animals are truly the American eagle like symbol of what's wild and wonderful about their Congo. Congolese who know of this animal greatly respect this gentle giant of the shadowy, cloud high hinterlands of what's left of the real Dark Continent. The Gorilla, besides being an animal of pride to the peoples there, is also a major tourist draw today, putting monies into their frail economy.

Fifty-two years later, I still treasure many of the items the pygmies gave us as special mementos of a trip into the past. Surely, if Gene and I had an H.G. Well's time machine, we could not have teleported ourselves back any farther into pre-history, than just traveling and living with the Pygmies of the Ituri rain forest. A few of these items can be described as priceless to me. One of them was a handmade knife I received as a gift that had a monkey skin sheath, was double edged and so sharp if I could have, I would have been able to shave with it. Another great item was a horn carved out of hippo tooth. It had a lizard skin cover near the mouth piece. It sounded out a loud higher pitched call than the big buffalo horn I was given. You could hear the call for miles in the jungle and it was the Pygmies cell telephone at that time in and in that place in time!

I traded for these items when I was in East and Central Africa. Each item has a special meaning for me as they were hand-crafted by peoples of the areas we met and visited with.

Eventually, we arrived in Stanleyville after spending a night in a small town northeast of this once bustling city. The bar we frequented had hookers of every description; it appeared that was the only work in town. We did not avail ourselves to the pleasures of the flesh however, for we felt that we didn't want to meet up with any wildlife that we could not easily see with our binoculars or even our bare eyes.

By this time, because of our diet of small, cold cans of Campbell's pork and beans, banana's, and whatever we could scrounge, along with an occasional twenty cent hot curried meal of fish, chicken, or mixed vegetables when we were able to find a small café restaurant that didn't have too many flies, we were literally becoming just skin and bones. Gene was so thin when we left Israel that he now looked emaciated, and his health began to deteriorate. I had some bulk on when we left Israel, so I just looked skinny (I had already lost over 40-pounds at this time). One of the interesting things we found, was that garlic was a very big deterrent to biting bugs, Han's really helped us out with this bit of information about the need and value of garlic. Garlic did not just keep the mosquito's at bay, but black flies, and a whole array of stinging and biting bugs that inhabit a land that never see's a killing frost, except for its highest mountains in Kenya such as Kilimanjaro.

In Stanleyville, we treated ourselves to a 2-dollar per night hotel. After a hot meal of rice and beans with a bit of chicken spiced to burn guts, we retired to our room. I was itching in my crotch region and so was Gene. After, we looked down in that region, we both discovered we had little tiny, but voracious crab lice. I freaked out! Gene was from Berkeley and already world wise. He said in the morning we'd buy a special cream at the pharmacy and they would go away. I could not wait. I went down to our Rover, siphoned some gas and took it up to the room. I poured gas on my private parts and began using a straight edge to shave off my hair. Gene yelled at me, but I was freaked out. I continued until my sensitive skin burned and I developed a serious rash. It was not a good night. Next morning, we got the cream, it worked! After driving around looking for a place to get an oil change-which we found and did, we noticed a memorial in the town square. It was for Lumumba, a communist sympathizer who much later on, I found out that he'd been killed by the CIA. Old man Stanley, of Stanley and Livingston fame, ("Mr. Livingston I presume") at that time, over 100-years passed, would not have liked his name-sake city. It was run down, the Simba (lion in Swahili) people filed their teeth, began taking over the city and began a roundup of whites. This preceded the UN mercenary air-lift of foreigners, who were being systematically rounded up, jailed, murdered-nuns were sliced up and fed to the crocodiles. We drove out just in time. A band of red-toothed Congolese were after us, but we beat them to the punch and were on our way to a rubber plantation to hide out and figure out how to get out of the Congo.

As I alluded to before, when we arrived in Dar Es Salam, Tanganyika, which was our last port of debarkation on the Pidanyunt ship, which continued on to South Africa, we found ourselves a hotel. We met a few British officers who were stationed in this incredibly beautiful port city, and they informed us that we were fool-hardy to try and attempted to cross Africa. We did not understand why they would say that until we arrived and found out that in almost every nation we visited there was both political and social unrest.

We were young and I was afraid, felt quite omnipotent at that time, as well as being imbued with a youthful exuberance, that also translated itself to a strong case of idealism. We were going to make everyone's lives brighter and better because we were Americans who cared for the peoples, flora and fauna of this great cradle of creation. Oh how foolish we were, but only to the extent that we did not fear for our lives, and had the naiveté of babes in arms. Just a few months later, reality began to "bite."

CHAPTER EIGHT

OUR STANLEYVILLE CONGO TIME ON THE WAY TO A GOODYEAR RUBBER PLANTATION

We left Stanleyville and continued heading towards Leopoldville, the capitol of the Congo. That first evening out of Stanleyville, after driving a hard and bouncing, 5-20-mph for hours, we spotted a run-down looking motor-court and decided to again sleep in a bed for at least one more night before heading into the hinterlands of jungle and veldts. We pulled in and a local who had taken over the motel court after the Belgian owners left in fear for their lives, approached us in the parking area. We asked him if he had a room for us and he offered us a room for 5-Congolese francs (at that time about a U.S. dollar). We took the Land Rover Key and our knapsack and checked in. First thing we noticed was the plumbing in the sink was gone, the door knob to the room was gone and no chain-lock was evident. Once we had our bananas with garlic for me (Gene couldn't stomach it) we looked out our French windows that opened out with a view of our Land Rover and settled into our beds. Since trading for my sword, I slept with my double edged sword very close and immediately reachable, this night was no different-we thought. I slept fitfully; Gene was soundly in la la land! At about midnight, I began having a nightmare-the image of my mother telling me I was in mortal danger and that if I did not wake-up and get out of the room, I would be slaughtered. I woke up at precisely 12:05 on this Wednesday night of our lives. The hair literally stood away from my neck-luckily, I believed that dream!

I immediately put my hand over Gene's mouth so he wouldn't call out in any way. I woke him up, no easy task that night! Gene slept well, except for when he was slapping at bugs that landed on him at night when we slept in our sleeping bags out on the road. I quietly stepped into my sandals and moved towards the door that I had jammed a chair against to keep it shut. I then heard muffled voices just outside the door. Gene was up and nearly paralyzed-he was scared stiff! I was not. Welling up in me was a giant charge of hormones charging up my body for fight or flight. Adrenalin almost had me floating out of my sandals. I drew my double edged sword and just as I did, the door was slammed and flew open breaking the chair back. Two men ran in with machetes. I sliced and diced at necks like a screaming banshee. I was covered in squirting blood from their fatal wounds. We (Gene and I) bailed out the French windows, taking the shortest distance between where we were and our vehicle was. As we ran towards the Land Rover we emerged from shading trees and in the moonlight saw several men standing at our vehicle with the engine hood up. Gene later told me that I put out a nerve shattering, hair curdling scream, as I ran headlong at the men who stood stiff and totally surprised at us not already being sushi in that room. They peeled away from the front of the Rover as I closed on them, and all but one, ran. I attacked that one. I was covered in blood and in the moonlight must have appeared to be quite a monster to this fellow too, as he began screaming and running away. I saw by the light of the moon that one of the battery cables was off the battery and the battery was already perched on top of the radiator. I lifted it with one hand by the remaining cable, dropped it into its little shelf, grabbed the other cable clamp and jammed it on the battery terminal and banged on it with my fist to make a firm connection; I did this with my right hand after shifting my sword to my left and weaker arm. We leaped into the rover, I found the key, hit the starter button and it sprung to life. As this occurred, here came the men I had frightened away. They must have seen the carnage and now they were out for blood, running at the vehicle and slashing at our top as we sped away without even turning on the driving lights, until I felt we were well away from that horror scene. I began to shake almost uncontrollably, my left foot danced spasmodically and I couldn't control it. Gene was practically catatonic; for it seemed an eternity in that first several miles after this incident of a lifetime or could have been a death time. Much later on in our trip, Gene confided in me with the following: "I truly believe that if you had not been with me on this trip, I'd be long dead now. The cost in having you along was more than paid for in spades-I'll never forget or doubt you again." Holy cow what an understatement-what else could he have said? Whatever he said at that time, would all have been an understatement! As we drove, I thought about all the could-have-happened: What if the men had pulled the distributor cap pulled off the spark plug wires, or any other way disabling the vehicle? Everything came down to timing for me at that time. Later, much later, many things got even weirder!

We arrived at a river crossing where we had to take a hand-pulled ferry barge. There were no bridges along the way fording most rivers in the Congo. This was just one of the more than a dozen we needed to take during our trip in the Congo. Gene prodded me about the blood on my shirt and before I had got out of the rover, I changed into cleaner T-shirt. Gene had already paid the boatman the 50-cents (as it came out in Congolese Francs) and then I relieved myself on a palm tree and drove the rover onto the barge. We were the only passengers. Once we got to the other side and started off again on our way to our intended visit to a leper colony that Gene wanted to visit and talk to the doctors there, I was relieved again. We were hours away from that horror show and I felt a whole lot better. I had a potato beer and celebrated. Umm! What can I say about warm potato beer, it even tasted pretty good, most other times ugh? But on second thought, according to my diary, this time it actually tasted great, after all, I/we still had our heads and could drink it when at other times it tasted terrible.

CHAPTER NINE

THE LEPER COLONY, FISHING, OUR RUBBER PLANTATION SOJOURN, A ROVER PLUNGE

We finally arrived at the Leper Colony and I was totally unprepared for what I was to experience there. We headed for a dingy looking bar which was the first building after we went through an open gate to the complex, which was really a little town housing very sick people. Gene spied another building, just to the rear of the bar, or if it was in Mexico; "cantina." According to my diary, I went in through two swinging doors into a dimly lit room. There was a typical looking bar with shelves holding various bottles, but no mirrors. At the bar sat a few men. I went to the bar and asked if they had beer. The bar keep said he did, but they had no refrigeration and it was potato beer, ugh! Just to my right sat what I thought was an old man. I made small talk with him and he turned towards me, the kerosene lantern light revealed his face to me and half of it was eaten away, the other half looked yellow, pallid and much younger than I thought at first. I definitely showed surprise! He offered me his half empty beer glass saying he had enough and he was being friendly. I gagged at the thought of drinking from his zombie-like lips. I thanked him, and left the bar. I know I disrespected him and still remember the dejection he showed me-a boy at 18, quickly becoming far older in experiential paradigms. I actually feel sorry about that moment to this day!

Leper colonies or houses became widespread in the middle ages, particularly in Europe and India, and often run by monastic orders. Historically, leprosy has been greatly feared because it causes visible disfigurement and disability, was incurable, and was commonly believed to be highly contagious. A leper colony administered by a Roman Catholic order was often called a lazar house, after Lazarus, the man that came back from the dead; the patron saint of lepers.

Some colonies like the one we visited were located on mountains or in remote locations in order to ensure quarantine, some were on main roads, where donations would be made for their upkeep. Debate exists over the conditions found within historical leper colonies; while they are currently thought to have been grim and neglected places, there are some indications that life within a leper colony or house was no worse than the life of other, non-quarantined individuals. There is even doubt that the current definition of leprosy can be retrospectively applied to the medieval condition. What was classified as leprosy then covers a wide range of skin conditions that would be classified as distinct afflictions today.

Some leper colonies issued their own money (such as tokens), in the belief that allowing lepers to handle regular money could spread the disease.

Gene made arrangements to visit with the doctor at the colony. After dropping Gene off at the Leper Colony, I decided to go fishing (Gene did get to go fishing with me the next day, too). I visited a little nearby village set next to a pretty jungle river scene. Dugout boats (hollowed out logs) were tied up and bobbed lightly in a small cove where young men and boys had been hanging around the area where they were just "killing time." When they saw my fishing gear, two boys of about 13 years in age jumped up off their log seats and offered to take me fishing. None of the boys ever saw a spinning reel and they were as curious about the gear as they were about me. After showing the boys how to use the reel and how they needed to be handle it so they can cast and retrieve the line and baits, they then began to fish. As I remember, they were quite fascinated by the reels and rods and especially the monofilament line. They were used to using hand lines that were woven out of plant fibers. Part of the tip that I offered to them was some fishing line from the future, their future! We caught tiger fish and tench (a type of carp) and took some pictures. I then decided that Gene would like this fishing experience and made a note to take him the next day. So the next day we went again (Gene and I) and met the same youths who had already created quite a stir, fishing with these guys (us) seemingly from outer space. We took on some celebrity status in that little village, and found that we had this experience continue in all the little hamlets and villages that we drove through. The weather was oppressively hot and steamy, so during our fishing trip we dove in to the water and had one of the boys take our picture holding fish for the photograph. The boys kept pointing to the banks and then we heard a huge splash as a giant crocodile launched itself from the river bank. Gene and I slid over the gunnels, back into the dugout as fast as we had jumped out of it! The boys laughed hard at our blatant stupidity! We laughed later once on terra firma. The dugout was quite unstable. If you made the wrong movements while you were inside and leaned too far over towards the boats, or if you leaned past the balance point of the boat, it was not a good move edge (much like a modern canoe). Heck, there were 15 foot, or larger saurian's hanging around, looking to pick off some appetizers. Gene wrapped up his visit and after stowing his writing folders (no computers in those days), we again headed towards our eventual run to Leopoldville, the Capitol of the Congo.

Each one of these pirogues or dugout canoes were hand made by hollowing out logs. Although heavy, we found them to be quite stable in calm backwater creeks and rivers.

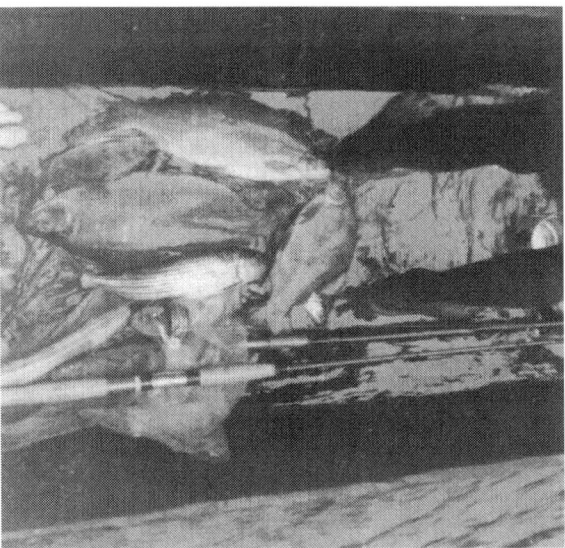

Tiger fish, tench, enough filets for a family of 10 in just 1-hour. We gave the fish to our young pirogue guides. They were thrilled that we thought of them with this bounty.

For the first time, this youngster was enthralled with our fishing reels and rods.

It was so humid that we still decided to take a swim even though the waters were filled with crocodiles and snakes. Our guides laughed at us. They thought we were funny and very crazy!

After our visit to this Leper Colony (at that time even as I was in the colony, I knew very little about what this disease really was) I believe that I should explain a bit about what Leprosy really is. Today, you don't hear much about Leper Colonies and probably not at all about this disease. There are many reasons for this; the biggest one is that the big 5-W's of Leprosy have been discovered (Gene was on the cutting edge of how to deal with Leprosy and prevent it). Leprosy through medical knowledge and research break-through is still a factor in the world today in maiming and greatly reducing the lifespan of those that contract it. I personally believe that AIDS became the disease de jour and bumped Leprosy down, as something the media would continue to report on. The 5-w's and big "H" are: Who gets it? What is it? Why does a person get it? When can it be contracted? Where is it most prevalent in the world? How do you get leprosy?

THE ORIGIN OF HANSEN'S DISEASE (LEPROSY)

"Leprosy has terrified humanity since ancient times and was reported as early as 600 BC in India, China, and Egypt. Hansen's disease is still a major health problem in many parts of Africa, Asia, and Latin America. For many centuries, leprosy was considered a curse of God, often associated with sin. It did not kill outright, but neither did it seem to end. Instead, leprosy lingered for years, causing the tissues to degenerate and deforming the body. Daniel Cornelius Danielssen who considered it a hereditary disease and had stated this in his book, "Traité de la Spedalskhed ou Elephantiasis des Grecs" - the standard reference book on leprosy from 1848 until the death of Danielssen in 1895. In 1867 Dr. Gavin Milroy finished the Royal College of Physicians' Report on leprosy. His work, which compiled data from all corners of the English empire, agreed with Danielssen that leprosy was a hereditary disease, but went further to state that leprosy was also a constitutional disease that could be mitigated by improvements in one's health, diet, and living conditions. When I was at the colony I was quite frightened by the prospect that I could contract this disease, however as I stated I knew very little about this pervasive disease.

Many as I did thought leprosy to be a disease of the skin. It is better classified, however, as a disease of the nervous system because the leprosy bacterium attacks the nerves. Leprosy's agent M. leprae is a rod-shaped bacterium related to the tuberculosis bacterium. Leprosy is spread by multiple skin contacts, as well as by droplets from the upper respiratory tracts, such as nasal secretions that are transmitted from person to person.

Its symptoms start in the skin and peripheral nervous system (outside the brain and spinal cord), then spread to other parts, such as the hands, feet, face, and earlobes. Patients with leprosy experience disfigurement of the skin and bones, twisting of the limbs, and curling of the fingers to form the characteristic claw hand. Facial changes include thickening of the outer ear and collapsing of the nose. I observed all of these symptoms that day at the bar.

Tumor-like growths called lepromas may form on the skin and in the respiratory tract, and the optic nerve may deteriorate. The largest numbers of deformities develop from loss of pain sensation due to extensive nerve damage. For instance, inattentive patients can pick up a cup of boiling water without flinching.

According to Dr. Brands findings, the best example in the Bible of a person with leprosy is the man with the withered hand (Mark 3:5; Matthew 12:13; Luke 6:10). He likely suffered from tuberculoid leprosy.

It was the work of Dr. Paul Brand (the late world-renowned orthopedic surgeon and leprosy physician) with leprosy patients that illustrated, in part, the value of sensing pain in this world. The leprosy bacillus destroys nerve endings that carry pain signals; therefore patients with advanced leprosy experience a total loss of physical pain. When these people cannot sense touch or pain, they tend to injure themselves or be unaware of injury caused by an outside agent.

In fact, some leprosy patients have had their fingers eaten by rats in their sleep because they were totally unaware of it happening; the lack of pain receptors could not warn them of the danger." _{Wikipedia} October 2013

A leper colony, leprosarium, or lazar (*as in Lazurus, who returned from the dead) house is a place to quarantine people with leprosy. There we were in a quarantined place, thanks to my traveling companion. I was not a happy camper at that time. One thing I knew was that I had signed on for a trip of a lifetime and Doc Gene was on a mission. I was part of that mission and today looking back, I would never want to miss that mission. However, at the time, my escape from it all was fishing. It was the only thing that could take my mind off of the thought of contracting this disease. At night during my rem sleep I dreamed of my fingers curling up and falling off, my nose melting and my eyes going dark. It took a long time to get those thoughts out of my head. Those thoughts lived there "rent free" for quite a long time.

When we left the Leper Colony, we ran into these 3 locals. They were entertainers and tale-talkers. They were practicing to be Witch Doctors. The two local Congolese on each end of the photo spoke French so they were able to translate for us!

AN UNEXPECTED RIVER PLUNGE WITH OUR ROVER

After finally leaving that leper colony, we drove for hours and then it started to get dark. Stopping in a small village, we had decided that we could still make some trip-time by going ahead until it was almost completely dark. Then we could find a spot to set up our sleeping bags for the night alongside the road. I had stopped along the way (I was always the driver) to wash my hands-probably washed my hands 10-times before getting to this village. I am sure today that what and where I washed my hands was probably more dangerous to my health than if I had just not bothered washing at all. Hindsight is funny sometimes!

My god! It's getting pitch black. We were deep in the hinterlands of the Congo. Suddenly, we took a plunge off of a log bridge. All of a sudden I felt dark swirling muddy water which quickly had been rising around my neck, and then the water was over my head. A moment before my mouth was covered, I yelled and screamed to Gene my traveling companion, "we're, dead, we're dead." In complete darkness, I kicked my way through the water out the open window on the driver's right side of our British Land Rover and Gene bailed out the other side. We made our way to a muddy bank. Then we crawled out and up through slippery vegetation climbing our way up the embankment that led to the dirt road that we had just been propelled from. This was another one of the most serious episodes that earmarked our travels through Africa. Wet, shook-up, and bedeviled immediately by the cacophony of frog peepers and coughs of jungle cats, we then made our way back towards a village that we had passed a few miles back. The questions that raced through my mind were: "Would we get out of this one? Would I ever see my mother and family again? Can we salvage the vehicle which was literally our lifeboat in a sea of seething uncertainty in a country that was in chaos and basically swimming in state of anarchy?

When we walked into this little town, there were about 20 men that were already standing around. One of men was holding a large coil of rope. It seems they knew all about our predicament just looking at our wet and muddy bodies. I am quite sure now, as I was then, that this was a trading opportunity for them. They offered to get our vehicle back on the road. They crawled and swam, tugged and slid that rover back up an embankment and back on the road again. Weird, but when we fell off the bridge the back of my hand slapped the key and broke it off. I had a gash on the back of my hand from the key and really never noticed the pain until I began walking to that village. Once we had the vehicle on the road again, we used a tweezers to pull the key out, inserted the spare, pressed the starter and our vehicle miraculously sputtered to life. We gave the 20 guys cigarettes and razor blades. They wanted no money. Either way it was, or went; they saved our butt that night!

I should explain that when we approached that jungle creek, the seedy grass was growing high in the middle of the road and as our front end hit the grass, it dislodged the seeds onto our soggy, dewy-damp windshield. We had limited visibility, so when we came to the two logs that was the bridge, one set of tires missed tracking true, and the tires did not line up to the center of the narrow logs, so the rover slid between the logs and crashed into the water.

We continued traveling to the rubber plantation after staying put for the night. We were probably more tired that night than any night since or before falling off the log. The next day and after miles of sweating it through humidity that hung in the air and everywhere and on everything in our life at that time, we eventually arrived at the Goodyear Rubber Plantation. The Plantation had been managed by a Mr. Goodman, from Holland. He put us up in a guest cottage. Goodman took us hunting for Dik Dik; jungle antelope as well as monkeys. He loaned us a 22-caliber rifle. We went out with two of his meat hunters and they carried a blunderbuss, which is an ancient Dutch bazooka style black powder monstrosity with a large flared barrel. The hunter poured nuts, bolts, nails and scrap iron pieces into the barrel. Then he poured in a charge of black powder and when we saw the first Dik- Dik, he let go with a boom and we recovered a mangled antelope for the pot as black smoke curled up into the tree canopy. I then popped a howler monkey for the brains. One of the hunters finished off the monkey I shot with a slam of its body against a tree, like the Pygmies had done. No one wanted to be bitten by a half dead monkey, their fangs were quite formidable and could cause much more than just a puncture wound! In any event any wound in the Congo could be extremely dangerous. The warm humid climate allowed bacterial action to often run rampant and there were few medicines available for treating any bites or accidental rupture of the saving membrane; ones skin! The next day we visited the rubber making operation. It was quite fascinating to see the beginning of a vehicle tire from white liquid latex sap dripping into a can to the final large, dense sheets of latex after boiling the sap. Later, much later in an industrialized nation to be turned into tires and other rubber products. It turned out; things were getting crazier by the day in the Congo. Dinner, with his wife and young child and all of us enjoying each other's company, Goodman announced that his wife and child would be leaving on the morrow for their safety. He proposed buying our Land Rover and hiding us in a latex truck and sending us to Lisala. We had driven through Lisala to reconnoiter where the river boat was and its schedules days before on our way to the plantation. Since that time, and while we were hunting and enjoying the hospitality of Goodman, things had gotten violent against whites. This was the port town where the riverboat to Leopoldville stopped once per week. We agreed and he paid Gene $500 for the Land Rover.

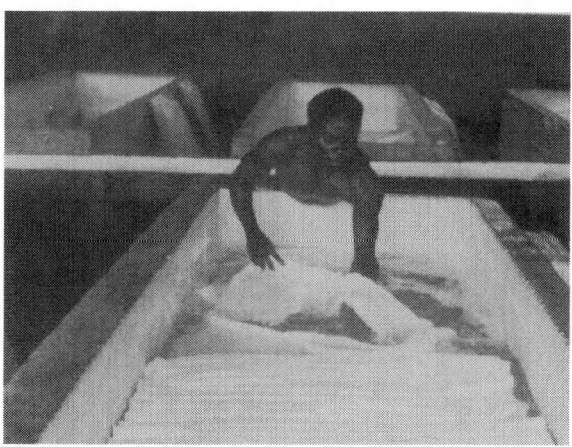

Latex were being processed into sheets at the plantation.

It was under these mats that we hid on the way to the Congo River.

We went hunting for monkeys and jungle antelopes with Goodman's rifle. His French made car had a sunroof and was a great hunting platform.

When one gets thirsty, a slice with a machete and a Liana vine that holds trapped rain water, makes for safe drinking.

My first monkey hunt. This monkey was served at the plantation for dinner. The dogs at my feet got it all. I couldn't eat monkey-they looked too much like babies when they are skinned and roasted.

Collecting latex sap from a rubber tree. A few slices on the tree bark and a path for the latex to run and drip into the catch-cup. Eventually this sap will roll along a road under an automobile or truck.

I stayed up late that night; I was intensely excited to finally begin the final process of heading home. By this time I was getting home sick and I wanted to again head over to the diner with my red and white Chrysler driving over paved roads and not having to look over my shoulder at who may be following us to do us harm.   The whole experience began taking a toll on my body, belief system and my nerves. Besides having lost over 52 pounds, I began dreaming of hot dogs and hamburgers with real bread buns, ketchup, french fries, ice cream with almonds. I could taste all this in my dreams. I was sick of bananas and little cans of Campbell's beans. I dreamed of my old girlfriend Ronnie, in the U.S. and Rouhama in Israel. I prayed in my dreams and on the road again as we traveled, that we would eventually make it home alive, or at the very least in one piece. I thought of my father; he had been in World War 2, jockeying a tank in the Battle of The Bulge in Belgium and what he must have gone through, eventually losing his toes on his right foot. He was captured by German soldiers just after a soldier ripped off his dog tags as he lay bleeding and in shock in a ditch. The dog tags said "Epstein" and had a Jewish star on it. He never would have made it home if the Nazi's saw this, instead he was taken to a German field hospital, sewed up and he survived to become my father after I was born in 1944. Sixty years later, I found out why my father never went swimming in the mountains of New York with the rest of the family. He was ashamed of his missing toes, so he would never take his shoes and socks off in front of me, my brother or for that matter, anyone else except my mother. She never told us either, why he never went in to swim with us during the heat of the summer. The next morning, our trip was a bit unnerving, as we laid under sheets of warm latex with our stuff and our bodies out of sight whenever we got to a checkpoint on the way to the Congo River.

In the Congo, as visitors we were looked upon as interlopers. This was not the case in the small villages, or with the peoples of the interior who were not sophisticated in the ways of the city folk who experienced firsthand the way colonialists did business. The following explains a bit about the history of the Congo that has helped understand why we were feared:

"When Portuguese explorer Daigo Cao discovered the mouth of the Congo River in 1482, it allowed Portugal to claim the region as its own. Until the middle of the 19th century, the Congo was at the heart of independent Africa, as European colonialists feared entering the interior. Along with very strong local resistance, the malaria breeding swamps and rainforests rife with various other diseases such as sleeping sickness, made it all quite impenetrable for Europeans to seriously consider visiting and conquering its environs to rape and pillage its possible resources. There were just no obvious economic benefits and the Congolese had quite a respite from western interference until 1876."

Health issues were seen everywhere. Goiter inflammations, all kinds of skin and extremities infested with various flukes and infections. The place made you want to become a doctor to help these people. But, it seems the witch doctors have their jobs cut out for them.

However, In 1876 Leopold II, King of the Belgians began a process that was to ultimately take the lives of fully 20-percent of the entire Congolese population, some 10-million of them at the time. He hosted a geographic conference in Brussels, inviting famous explorers, philanthropists, and members of geographic societies to stir up interest in a "humanitarian" endeavor for Europeans to take in central Africa so as to improve and civilize the lives of the indigenous peoples. At the conference, Leopold organized the International African Association with the cooperation of European and American explorers and the support of several European governments, and was himself elected chairman. Leopold used the Association for the promotion of plans to seize independent Central Africa under this philanthropic guise. In more modern times, more people have died in the Congo than anywhere else since World War 11, more than 5.5 million more than 90-percent of the deaths are from malnutrition and lack of access to health care. Att:(Marcus Bleasdale, The Moment, National Geographic October 2013) this is not to say that the does not include the thousands of other deaths that have occurred within Rebel rivalries and sectarian war. Bleasdale said that he also had the experience of being stopped by a rebel group on the road and detained for one day. Because we could speak French we were able to communicate a bit stronger and only spent an hour in detention with the rebels that stopped us in 1963.

"Henry Morton Stanley, famous for making contact with British missionary David Livingstone in Africa in 1871, had later explored the region during a journey that ended in 1877 described in Stanley's novel Through the Dark Continent (1878). Failing to enlist British interests in the development of the Congo region, Stanley took service with the Leopold II, who hired him to help the king to gain a foothold in the region and secretly wished to annex the region for himself. From August 1879 to June 1884 Stanley was in the Congo basin, where he built a road from the lower Congo up to Stanley Pool and launched steamers on the upper river. While exploring the Congo for Leopold, Stanley set up treaties with the local chiefs and with native leaders. Few to none of these tribal leaders had a realistic idea of what they were signing, and, in essence, the documents gave over all rights of their respective pieces of land to King Leopold II. With Stanley's help, Leopold was able to claim a great area along the Congo, and military posts were established.

Christian de Bonchamps, a French explorer who served Leopold in Katanga, expressed attitudes towards such treaties shared by many Europeans, saying, "The treaties with these little African tyrants, which generally consist of four long pages of which they do not understand a word, and to which they sign a cross in order to have peace and to receive gifts, are really only serious matters for the European powers, in the event of disputes over the territories. They do not concern the black sovereign who signs them for a moment." So it is part of history that Leopold II, King of the Belgians was the de facto owner of the Congo Free State from 1885 to 1908.

In 1885, Leopold began to carefully create a plan to convince other European powers of the legitimacy of his claim to the region, all while maintaining the guise that his work was for the benefit of the native peoples under the name of a philanthropic "Association". His desire for territory and colonial control in Africa is evident when Leopold stated:

"I do not want to risk...losing a fine chance to secure for ourselves a slice of this magnificent African cake" so it was reported to one of his aids in London." Wikipedia information-October-2013

On the road again, we met this very friendly group of men in just one more no- name village along our way through the Congo. They were proud of the boa snakeskin and wanted us to take a picture of it.

CHAPTER TEN

LEOPOLDVILLE AND THE CONGO

We made it without incident to the port town of Lisala on the Congo River. Gene and I walked the road area near the river, took photographs, checked out the interesting sights such as on one small dock contained the body of a giant catfish. It was an over 500-pound catfish. The mouth was large enough to swallow a child for sure!

The fish laid out on a dock and blow -fly larvae squirmed in an open slice on the rotting fish. Big, white larvae were being picked out of the fish by children who called them "ascreem" they ate them up and I was offered one, served on a leaf by one of the youngsters. I took it and put it on my hook for bait. The kid laughed heartily. I caught a nice fat fish and gave it to the youngster. He acted like he won the lottery, showing it off and bragging to his little friends.

While in Lisala, near the ticket office for the boat, we met a Belgian man. He offered us his help to get tickets and assist us to get onto the boat. He told us that if we did not have his help, he said that the managers of the office selling tickets would gouge us harshly. They may not even let us get tickets or perhaps break our bank roll. Everything was "bock-shish" (bribery) in the Congo. We thanked him, and then we hung around for hours trying to get on the boat.

Finally, we boarded and left the Lisala docks on the "boat"; a riverboat pushing a huge barge a microcosm of African life. It was being pushed along by a 2000 horsepower diesel engine turning a paddlewheel that splashed at the river and inexorably pushed more than 1000 souls along a river that hasn't changed since or before written history, one iota. Congolese minister's concubines took up most of the riverboat rooms. Gene and I got lucky enough with the help of a Belgian business man, to grab one of those rooms. God had mercy; we did not have to sleep on the deck with the water bugs and other slimy critters that came out on deck under cover of darkness. We settled in for a ten day run to Leopoldville. I spent a lot of time on the barge. I just could not read a book that I wanted to finish because there was too much to absorb. So many things were kaleidoscopically passing by my eyes almost every moment of the trip. I visited the Cayman croc sellers, the fruit and vegetable vendors and looked over the booty and bounty of what many villagers had bagged in the jungles hinterlands including: smoked monkeys, boa constrictor snakes for food, or sale to collectors, butterflies kept in-between palm leaves also for the collector. There was also raw latex from Goodman's Goodyear rubber plantation on its way to be processed into gloves, tires, rubber boots, and condoms. Additionally, there were wildly colorful songbirds and parrots, snakes, monkeys and sloths, bamboo and logs destined for trading in the capitol of the Congo, Leopoldville.

As we passed through various villages, I always asked locals if I could photograph them for the memories. They mostly allowed me to do this without much fuss except sometimes, for a few Francs or cigarettes.

A Congolese houseboat. An entire family lived in this boat. I counted 6 men, women and children.

Youngsters walking the road alongside the Congo River in Lisala, Congo.

We reconnoitered the travel options alongside the Congo River.

As we sailed along the Congo, various vendors came alongside by dugout to sell fresh vegetables and fruits. My favorite was sugar cane.

Every minute was an adventure on the riverboat. Villagers, whose huts hugged the river banks along the way, braved the boats wake and came out to the barge in "pirogues" hollowed out, log dugout canoes. They traded fresh produce, including cut pieces of sugar cane a favorite treat for everyone aboard. If you wanted Bangui or little red bananas, a monkey for roasting, a snake for same, natural woven baskets, or stained baskets with little geometrical designs-a whole array of various handmade wood and ivory, carved items, you could get them. Various skins of jungle animals were also offered, chervil cats, monkey skins, goat skins and snake skins, basically many of the items already brought on the barge to be sold in Leopoldville.

All the things done in the village were being accomplished on the barge as it was pushed at about at 5 mph towards Leopoldville. On the shade of the decks behind a cloth shade or out in the open, everyday tasks such as: clothes washing, sleeping, cooking, child care and even love making was going on. A stroll around the decks allowed for viewing a little microcosm of how these Congolese people lived when back in their land-based villages. They were basket weaving mats being woven, babies being breast fed, men carving wood images of women, animals, various African scenes such as palm trees and the river itself. There were cages of chickens, pea hens, nutria, snakes, crocodiles, and monkeys and all manner o fruits and vegetables. Bound rolls of cut bamboo and also hard-wood boards and various and sundry goods for sale and trade. If you wanted hashish, you could get it. I was through by that time ever messing with drugs again. My Uganda horror of nearly losing my mind for good taught me that lesson. This deepest of rivers of the world meanders softly, but carries a mighty huge stick and a kick! The villages we passed, were mostly on stilts near the river-on stilts due to the fact that the river does overflow it's banks many times reaching heights of 20-feet above the main bank of the river and moving deep into the jungle interiors. From viewing my diary as I write this, I now remember how green everything was, how dense and overpowering the aromas of the various river side foliage were. All the boats were carved out of logs, thus called dugouts and were propelled by men and women with very long poles. None of the dugouts, venturing very far from shore. Their poles wouldn't reach the bottom that is over 1000-feet in the center of the river.

Near a large net drying between two poles I asked a passing lady if she would let me take a picture of her. She smiled and put out her palm for a franc coin. She, as all the women I saw carried their goods on their heads. This one struck a particularly fine pose. She was who she was; a beautiful Congolese woman.

One of our stops was at a river front town of Coquilhatville to pick up various produce goods and tropical jungle woods. There was a long daylight stopover there, so we walked into a very picturesque town which was very close to the docks. There were only three dusty roads in that town. Today, there is an airport, a printing plant and I hear air conditioning in a few of the buildings. In 1962, there was only a small country store and decided to see what we could buy for snacks, bottled drinks and meals. Going in to the store, we met a German gent and he took great interest in us. He asked us how we were able to be making this trip safely with all the unrest and turmoil in the country. We told him a bit about our trip and he asked us if we would like to have dinner at his club and meet his pals? He said it would be early enough so we could easily have enough time to get back on our boat.

We accepted. He pointed out the clubhouse building which was located about 1000-feet away from this store that we were in. After buying some boxes of crackers and cans of Belgian onion soups (all they had left in the store of mostly bare shelves), we stowed our stuff back on the boat, took a walk looking at unreal orchids and flowering trees and plants in this equatorial jungle town in the Congo and headed for the German's clubhouse. When after entering the clubhouse, we almost choked when we viewed the pictures that were hanging prominently on the walls. There was a big painting of Hitler, and a rogue's gallery of his henchmen's pictures. Additionally, the walls were painted with things that included a giant swastika flag next to the Congolese flag. As soon as I saw these things, I began backing out the door and Gene stopped me. He said; "Bob, this should be very interesting." Well it was! A number of men began filing in to the club house and all tipped their straw hats at us. We sat near the head of the table and frankly, the feeling had been very eerie. We were asked lots of questions which concerned our trip. One such question was: "What was going on in Stanleyville with the communists?" Another question asked was: "How did we make it from the Rwanda/Burundi border this far and still kept our skins on?" Another question asked was "Why this trip, where had we been along the way?" etc. and so it went on. The cook began bringing in food products and a large silver hot server was set in front of me and Gene. When they took the cover off, there sat a roasted monkey. It really looked like a roasted child or Pygmy. It was horrible. There was no way could I eat this dish. Apparently these Germans got a big kick from my surprise and laughed with big guffaws. I felt that if they could get away with it, they would do it to us. After looking at the dish, I knew they would. We had fallen into a nest of escaped Nazi's, for sure! At that point, we thanked them and took a rather quick leave of absence-heading for the boat rather quickly. We then showered in our cabin (in tepid water) and had bananas, mango, and guava for dinner. Our dessert was sweet sugar cane to chew on. After dinner, Gene and I looked out at a setting sun with a warm, yet cooling and comforting breeze, as dugout canoes slid by, poled by lithe, muscular

146

men. They were plying their trades of selling and trading sugar cane, fruits and vegetables to many travelers on our barge and push paddle wheeler.

Upon our return home to the United States, I had told many of our experience with these Germans to various authorities in the U.S.A. They told us that they would never be able to get to them, even if I was right. They said after all; "they were in the Darkest Africa, the Congo and I had no names or images of the Germans we met." (From my diary)

CHAPTER ELEVEN

LEOPOLDVILLE: THE AMERICAN AND THE ISRAELI EMBASSIES

The last boat line was dropped off the dock piling and the paddle wheeler began pushing our barge towards Leopoldville once again. The darkness eventually became complete after the last rays of the suns glow was hidden by the dense foliage on each side of this huge river. By nine pm it was dark, very dark, yet there were streaks of color in the very shadowy clouds still visible. The omnipresent sound of the paddlewheel making a rhythmic, whooshing sound soon became light background cadence to the singing, and drumming on the barge. Sitting out on wicker chairs outside our cabin, we took in the sights and sounds below us on the barge and it was remarkably entertaining. No TV or radio could have had more impact than the people of another time and place from ours, going about their daily and nightly business, pursuing their lives.

Eventually, after a 10-day cruise we arrived in Leopoldville. Leopoldville, which was the capitol of the Congo De Belgique (the name at the time, beware of countries that keep changing their name). We had gone back to our cabin after visiting the little restaurant on board the paddle wheeler and found that we had been robbed again.

This time someone grabbed our American Express Travelers Checks. They did not get our passports-we got lucky! So as soon as we could after debarking, we went to the American Embassy, after putting in for check replacements which would take a week to get. We had no money, so we could not get a room. At the Embassy, we were able to talk to the Ambassadors assistant and told him of our plight. We asked him if they could assist us with a few dollars, we then would be able to rent a hotel room and feed ourselves until our traveler's checks were replaced. He looked at our U.S. Passport and said: "We cannot help hippies that come in here for money. I see on your passport that you were in Israel. So go to the Israeli Embassy and maybe they would help you, we will not." Gene and I were quite incensed over this, but all I said was "someday if you live long enough, (he was in his 50's) you'll read about this and how we were treated and you will remember and be very sorry." He's gone now unless he's over 90-years old! So we did, we left and walked over to the Israeli Embassy. We were greeted wonderfully! The Ambassador told us that the Israeli Military Attaché' had a huge apartment and he would call her and ask her if she could take us in for the week. He did and she did! A wonderful lady in her 20's absolutely gorgeous redhead greeted us at her door, made us feel very welcome, and saw us to the two spare bedrooms and bathroom. After discussing our adventures with her, she told us that she was inviting us to an Ambassadors dinner that night. She felt they would like to talk to us about Stanleyville, the Simba (Lion) terrorists, the killing of Priest Johnson, the nuns being fed to the crocodiles and how in the heck we made it through there alive. And besides, the food would be great! We were on for the night! She gave us some clothes belonging to her boyfriend, the Nigerian Military Attaché' and two pairs of his shoes. We showered with warm water for the first time in months, using soap and real shampoo. I even shaved for the first time too! That evening we were basically interrogated by the Russian, American, British (the British Ambassadors wife had been killed the week before due to being out on the road after curfew and she was summarily shot by a Congolese soldier) Ambassadors. I recall stuffing myself with hors douvres, later to be sick to my stomach not being used to such rich and refined food. By the time we left on a Pan Am Jet, I had lost over 56-pounds since leaving Israel. Gene looked like a Holocaust survivor. We spent a fine week waiting for Gene's Ford Foundation American Express Checks to come in, the 500-dollars paid in British pounds by the Dutchman Goodman was also stolen, that, we never did recover. The Israeli lady took care of all of our food and accommodations and asked for nothing but a smile. We loved her! We were warned not to walk around Leopoldville without an armed guard, so we mostly stayed at the apartment, read magazines and I was able to read magazines in Hebrew compliments of Elihana, our apartment hostess.

Finally our checks came in. We bought tickets for a flight to New York's, La Guardia Airport with stopovers, in Nigeria, Senegal, the Ivory Coast and Ghana. Gene was becoming ill. I thought he had the flu. I was a bit weak, but I really believe that garlic kept me in good stead, health wise. During that dinner, the Ambassadors asked me why I had an odor of garlic surrounding me, and I told them a Nazi war criminal taught me about all things garlic to ward of plague, cholera, and every other flying or crawling bug that lives. They got a big laugh over that comment. I'm sure they didn't believe me.

CHAPTER TWELVE

FLIGHT HOME ON PAN AM TO NEW YORK

We were driven to the airport by Elihana, our dear new Israeli friend, who helped us in Leopoldville. We kissed her goodbye; she is someone I will never forget. When we got to the airport and after checking in, two very large muscular Congolese border guards said "come with us and bring all your things." They looked like the swordsman from hell-very scary looks on their wide coal-black faces, and gleaming muscular arms. I tried to stay composed, but when they asked us if we had any contraband, diamonds, gold, the memory of that little Chinese gal and Hans came top- of- the-mind instantly and I said "no!" With a giant sigh of relief, I looked at Gene and said "see they were right" as one of the big guys stuck a rubber gloved finger up my rear-end. Our armpits, mouths and any crevice were searched for contraband. Our toothpaste that we just were given by Elihana was squeezed out; all our things were searched and thrown about. They found nothing except ivory crocodiles and spears, swords, masks (in those days this stuff was considered trash by these people, to us high collectibles). They opened the door and one of the two men said cryptically: "You two lucky white boys, yesterday we sent a white boy to prison." We found out later and already more or less knew; that you don't leave a Congolese prison alive, they murder you for your flip flops or you die of disease!

Eventually, after arriving back in the USA and getting off our quarantined Pan Am Jet, while waiting for doctors checking all of us after a Cholera epidemic had broken out during our trip in Ghana; one of our stopovers on our way home from Leopoldville, I finally realized I was home. As I peered out the window, I saw my family and friends under a banner that read: "Welcome Home Bwana Bob." However, the shock of my life still awaited me. It was about to unfold at my home in Queens, New York. After arriving home and showering, eating a bit of spaghetti and a slice of apple pie with real ice cream, my mother and I compared our diaries. Mom had a paragraph that outlined the threat I was under-how she awoke and prayed I'd be OK! Her premonition was under the banner and time of precisely the 12-hour world- time difference when that horrific incident in the motel, occurred. Our diary entries matched for day and time! She had called the BBC Network to put out an alert for me. I never heard anything from the BBC. But, the time that I had awakened from a dream that my mother warned me of imminent danger, my hair standing up on the back of my neck, the feeling that what she warned me about was real and it was, so from that day on, I truly began believing in G-D! I believe today that my mother somehow was telepathically protecting and warning her son, thousands of miles away, it had convinced me there was more to this life for all of us, than just striving for money and trying to win by dying with the most toys! That was the day of all days that the word "prayer" although I had prayed many time in the Congo (Africa on a Pin & a Prayer) became important to me. I also took away the following: readiness, the true element of surprise, the right tool and the instant willingness to do what must be done without hesitation, can save your life and the life of others with you. Like a fire, that requires heat, oxygen and fuel, if one of those elements just mentioned were missing, I would not be writing this book!

I take comfort from my Israeli family of peoples and their government in readiness, that they follow the above description of how to meet head-on and more importantly, pre-empt any true dangers the state of Israel faces daily, even minute by minute. But, I will say; it really is up to "Ha Shemesh" (the one G-D) in the heavens and all of us, and in everything; G-D is actually, what becomes the reality of the day and the next, and onto the next day! I arrived home and it hit me that my girlfriend, when I had left for Israel, waited for me to return for many months, then found a new boyfriend, many of my friends had moved on, my wonderful brother Mike had used my car a 55-Chrysler and threw it in reverse while the vehicle was going in drive. When I finally arrived home, I had to park the Chrysler so I didn't have to back up anymore. On the most positive note, my brother Mike also introduced me to my wife of nearly 5-decades, now. I think, and at the time as well, that he made up for wrecking my old Chrysler. I soon found a rag-top 1961 Volkswagen and gave my Chrysler to my brother. He deserved it! I began dating Barbara within two months of my returning home and all during my 4-year stint in college. We married at the end of my last year in college. I got lucky, real lucky, but don't ask Barbara if she did! We lived in Vermont and I taught a 5th grade class in science and English for a year and then we decided 25-below was just too cold for us.

We moved our family; David our oldest and Brian our baby to the Florida Keys in 1977. They were brought up in the Keys and never ate any old fish or seafood again. I wrote for local papers, freelanced over the years more than 2500 articles and had over 5000 images published nationally and internationally. The children grew up; one went to the Air Force and the other into the steel & news industry. My focus, or should I say our focus has been in travel and food writing for the past 15-years, but I am still creating and selling fishing and assorted outdoor articles. I wrote nine books and this one is my absolute favorite. It has taken a half of century to finally finish it. So here it is, you've read it all I hope, and please give me your feedback! Thanks for opening a small window into my life!

RUMINATIONS:

THIS IS MY LIFE SO I GET TO SAY WHAT I WANT ABOUT THE AUTHOR!

During those times in my life, living in Africa, there were times when I thought the whole world was going mad and then I thought, no not yet. It was a time before Vietnam, after Korea, and President Kennedy had told the Russians to "blink" before there was war during the Cuban Missile crisis. They did!

Overall at that time, peace reigned in America, though a seething discontent was growing. Negroes, as they were called at that time in the U.S., today Blacks, wanted more of the "American pie", they felt they deserved better than what they had. Many also thought they were owed a huge apology for treatment they received as slaves and throughout the South after their forefathers were emancipated. "Affirmative Action" became the law of the land-reverse discrimination was rampant! These beliefs were simmering under, and began boiling over the surface like hot magma, finally released from its pressure-cooker earth confines. When I got home, President Kennedy, M.L. King and Kennedy's brother, Bobby had been murdered. There were riots, and much strife in my country. One thing we, the U.S.A., had, I thought was a common language-it didn't matter who and where we were, there was good communication if one merely participated in it. Even with everyone speaking English, not everyone was communicating effectively. In Africa there were so many different languages, so many dialects (that like the Tower of Babel in biblical times), Africans from one country never mind district, in their same country could not easily communicate with one another. I saw this again and again and I was just a teenager at the time! At that time; 52-years ago, I decided I wanted to become a writer. I took it to heart that "the pen was mightier than the sword." The sword for an instant cut away the problem, but whatever that savagery wrought, it reincarnated again and again. The pen made a much different indelible mark, irrefutable, forever, wherever people, books and manuscripts were not burned by that sword. Before Africa, I had no desire to go to a formal education place; I felt I could just travel my whole life gleaning an education by just traveling the world away, but Africa and those continuous voids, incriminations, pogroms I encountered between those peoples, made me realize I needed the tools necessary to "communicate"! I resolved if and when I could, I would go to a college or University, acquire more of the tools that I would need to make it through this life, make it better for me and mine and communicate how others can, or at least being able to make sense of, and offer that information to whoever wanted it. I'll always keep trying to do this in my various communication venues! Today hundreds of thousands have read my relatively new WWW.APtravelnews.com travel, adventure and food daily posts!

In Windham College, located in Putney, Vermont I was also involved in the Drama Club. Our professor handling this club asked me to be Kipling for an Evening, in a Kipling show he had planned and advertised in the newspapers and college paper as well. He said I would be memorizing poems and stories, and be dressing as Kipling would have in his day, during my presentations. I studied for this and the whole evening came off very well. I even had glowing reviews in the newspapers. I was asked by the father of local (soon to be a debutante and friend of Kathleen Kennedy, who was in the audience, coming from The School for International Living and the Putney School which she attended) if I wanted to meet with a movie director friend who worked with Actor Dreyfus on a project? (She did not know that I already knew Dreyfus) I told her no thanks! I really never wanted to become an actor, I never wanted to be on call for anything other than what I felt was important and acting (mimicking reality) was not to me, an important profession, although worth its weight in gold if one becomes successful. I am not sorry all these years later that I turned this potential opportunity down except for the money and fame that could have come to me and my family, but my uncle Bill always told me "never do things just for the money, only do them because you have a passion to do it, if you do, the money will eventually come to you too." I've always listened to that advice and lived by it. So, all things I do, including this book is because I have that "passion" my Uncle Bill Brenner told me to live by. By the way; Uncle Bill, an Engineer is also a well known inventor. He only invented things that help people live better lives and he's succeeded all the way as a fantastic father, to a doctor, nurse and teacher, a husband to Rose my terrific aunt, grandfather and my incredible uncle, too!

I think that since I believe I owe that "stinking rose" my life, I believe I would like to open a restaurant that features dishes steeped in garlic; offering the world; "grub fragrance." Just down the road from my home in Port St. Lucie, West, in New Smyrna Beach, Florida, lives a restaurant called The Garlic, real Tuscan delights. Other restaurants in the U.S.A. are the Stinking Rose in San Francisco and a garlic specialty restaurant in Colorado, such as Garlic Mikes and in Philadelphia, Pennsylvania; Jakes offers the "Garlic Bomb." My restaurant would be called Bob's Allium Emporium I'd sneak into the business and not let the name over power the garlic themes. I think I'm moving to the Garlic Capitol of the world; Gilroy, California. Everything garlic- 5-tons of it gets eaten at Gourmet Alley in Gilroy during the festival. Come join me; I'm heading there now!

Printed in Great Britain
by Amazon.co.uk, Ltd.,
Marston Gate.